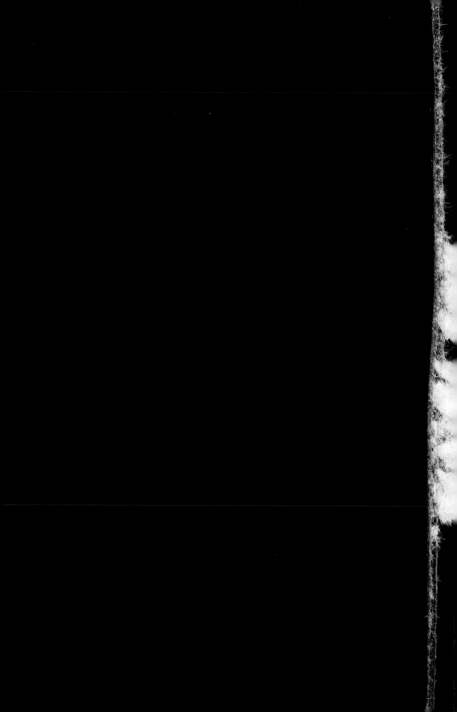

AN ABOLITIONIST'S HANDBOOK

Also by Patrisse Cullors

When They Call You a Terrorist: A Story of Black Lives Matter and the Power to Change the World

When They Call You a Terrorist: A Black Lives Matter Memoir

AN
ABOLITIONIST'S
HANDBOOK

12 STEPS TO CHANGING
YOURSELF AND the WORLD

PATRISSE CULLORS

ST. MARTIN'S PRESS
NEW YORK

First published in the United States by St. Martin's Press, an imprint
of St. Martin's Publishing Group

AN ABOLITIONIST'S HANDBOOK. Copyright © 2021 by Patrisse Cullors.
All rights reserved. Printed in the United States of America.
For information, address St. Martin's Publishing Group,
120 Broadway, New York, NY 10271.

www.stmartins.com

Library of Congress Cataloging-in-Publication Data

Names: Khan-Cullors, Patrisse, 1984- author.
Title: An abolitionist's handbook : 12 steps to changing yourself
　　and the world / Patrisse Cullors.
Description: First edition. | New York : St. Martin's Press, 2021. |
　　Includes bibliographical references.
Identifiers: LCCN 2021021151 | ISBN 9781250272973 (hardcover) |
　　ISBN 9781250280657 (signed) | ISBN 9781250272980 (ebook)
Subjects: LCSH: Alternatives to imprisonment. | Prisons—Moral
　　and ethical aspects. | Prison abolition movements. |
　　Prison-industrial complex.
Classification: LCC HV9276.5 .K43 2021 | DDC 364.6—dc23
LC record available at https://lccn.loc.gov/2021021151

Our books may be purchased in bulk for promotional, educational,
or business use. Please contact your local bookseller or the Macmillan
Corporate and Premium Sales Department at 1-800-221-7945,
extension 5442, or by email at
MacmillanSpecialMarkets@macmillan.com.

First Edition: 2021

10　9　8　7　6　5　4　3　2　1

I dedicate this book to every single person fighting for a world without cages, police and surveillance, but also fighting for a world where accountability isn't about punishment but rather about transformation and dignity.

Contents

Foreword

ADRIENNE MAREE BROWN

Patrisse Cullors wants you to know that abolition is vulnerable, intimate, personal and non-negotiable work.

As I write this to you, the cry to "defund the police" rises up in chorus around the world—one way that the public is evolving the discourse with the ideas of abolition. There are experiments in redistributing budgets from policing and incarceration to the more effective long-term strategies of mental health support, mediation and conflict resolution. There are articles in every major paper and magazine debating just how literally we as abolitionists mean for the general public to interpret these three words. And we answer, singing in assertion of our vision: yes, we mean an end of police; yes, we mean the end of prisons. Yes, we are saying that the hypothesis that prisons and policing keep us safe has been disproved, and we are ready to learn what will actually work at the scale of relationship. Communities are reckoning with the responsibility of embodying abolition in our intimate and neighborhood relationships, in how we navigate conflict within our movements, in how we understand our very identities.

Abolition is a series of choices and practices. Throughout history, to stand with abolition has meant to move toward liberation by escaping and running for freedom, to hide people in your home, to intervene in the efforts of the slaver and slave catcher and in more recent years to develop an analysis of the throughline from slavery to the prison-industrial complex. Deeply personal choices can create a pattern of abolition. And in this moment, we are understanding, more deeply than ever, that each of us is called to the work of self and collective transformation for a future that abolition has helped create.

We can't get where we need to go if we aren't willing to be vulnerable, to make mistakes, to recognize inside of ourselves the capacity to misstep, to act in anger and reaction, to lose touch with our good intentions. And then—and this is the important part—to turn and face those missteps with humility and curiosity, allowing those difficult moments to become the skeletal structure for our integrity and dignity, for our political clarity.

In the pages that follow, Patrisse owns her own missteps and reactions, and claims her lessons, bringing us all into the courageous conversation. Before she was a co-founder of Black Lives Matter, Patrisse was already an abolitionist working to transform the conditions of her community, impacted by her own familial experiences with the carceral state. She has already given us the memoir *When They Call You a Terrorist,* and in *An*

Abolitionist's Handbook she builds a bridge from her story to our own, from our challenges to our hardest-won lessons, from our dysfunctional system to accessible practices we can all put into application for our collective abolitionist journey. Patrisse weaves her abolitionist story into a fabric thick with ancestors and comrades—Ida B. Wells, Eleanor Bumpurs, bell hooks, Cara Page, Leah Lakshmi Piepzna-Samarasinha, Mia Mingus, Prentis Hemphill, Ruthie Wilson Gilmore and many more.

Patrisse honors her lineage as she shows us where and how she learned to navigate vulnerability and need. We get to learn from the ways she has loved and fought and stayed in the work and from her personal and political relationships. From her journey through a Jehovah's Witness upbringing into a queer polyamorous adulthood, her journey from daughter to mother, her journey from family member of incarcerated Black humans to organizer transforming the conditions of liberation and her balancing between activism and cultural work, we get to see the constant forces of change. We get to learn from Patrisse how we can harness the energy of change toward our best selves, and toward our inevitable abolitionist future.

Introduction

PRENTIS HEMPHILL

I met Patrisse many years ago around the same time I was introduced to abolition. I met her (her father, too) at a fundraiser for a mutual friend's brother who had just recently been incarcerated. I have several family members who have been incarcerated. One, a cousin, was inside at the time, and I was beginning to politically engage in organizing efforts around opposing jail expansion. I was on the cusp of bringing the important, necessary worlds together inside of me: my personal life and story and my organizing visions. That night, with the openness and clarity with which everyone spoke about the interconnection between the two and the out loud dreaming of another way for our relations, was a revelation to me. Abolition was no longer something that happened outside of me or far away from me. I could also now see how abolition meant new futures for my family and for all of our families.

That abolition has come to be a more mainstream debate and conversation, and that it has finally moved beyond the margins of the impossible, is a testament mostly to the work of organizers and scholars who have been telling the truth about our systems for decades. Change can start to happen when we stop taking for granted the confines of our reality and start to become responsive to the lessons we are learning. Abolition is that call, that catalyst. For many this may be a new awakening, a realization that through all the concepts of punishment, and all the stated logic of incarceration, we have been unable to address what seems fundamentally most important when something goes wrong: healing, repair and transformation. In fact, we are realizing that our current systems leave breaches and pain greater than what existed before and equally as tragic. Our current systems of punishment accelerate the ills of history, capturing the poor, the Black, the Brown, the disabled. We can and we have to do better.

This offering from Patrisse Cullors is a gift to those ready to practice abolition. It is a guidebook, a back-pocket reference when you need it. It is also a reminder that the transformation of systems happens in our most intimate places as much as anywhere else. How we deal with the breakdowns with our own people is a demonstration of what we have embodied up to this point. In this book, we are given permission to be in development, to be in learning and practice. We have a long way to go and this is a meaningful move forward for all of us wanting to make the impossible real.

Along the way you will get to hear Patrisse's reflections, her navigation of complex scenarios, her reflection through story of what this work means and looks like on the ground. She lets us in on where she comes from and who has inspired her along the way. It is so important to name our teachers and co-learners. These are reminders that we are not alone right now or in history. We have and are creating a lineage linked together by a commitment to freedom, but more specifically, we are creating systems that are human centered, repair and healing centered. Systems that believe in the greatest potential of human beings even when we mess up. This book is a companion for all of us in imagining and practicing something more beautiful and more just.

AN ABOLITIONIST'S HANDBOOK

What Is a Handbook?

Handbook (noun):
a. A book capable of being conveniently carried as a ready reference.
b. A concise reference book covering a particular subject.

What you're holding is not meant to live on a bookshelf. It's not a textbook, meant for a semester or some singular moment in time. It's not meant to serve as a backdrop for a conference call. My goal is this: The things I've learned about the work I'm in can be valuable. Once you gain a certain sense of self about a particular part of your life, the best thing to do next is to share it.

That's what this handbook is.

After 20 years of organizing and movement work, I've seen and experienced quite a bit: the good, the bad and the ugly, from myself and others. A few years ago, I developed 12 principles or steps that I believe are an essential framework to grow and develop as an abolitionist. I put these ideas into practice, taking great pains to try to maintain my commitment. It's not easy, but it's been worth it.

This book is not meant to prove to someone who you are—or who you aren't. Carrying this book won't scream, *I'm an abolitionist!* Not carrying it won't scream that you're not one, either.

This book won't remain spotless. It will have notes scribbled in the margins, questions and reminders for yourself and others. I hope this book makes you think. I don't need you to always agree with my thoughts here. If I've done my job, you *won't* agree with every line.

You'll disagree on some points, sometimes vehemently. Use bookmarks and highlighters. Come back to ideas and reread them if it moves you to do so. Share this book. If there's an idea or narrative or dynamic that you think applies to someone you think could benefit from it, let them know.

However, there are some things I need you to understand before we begin. First, this is not a memoir. I did that. I'm proud of it. My mission is not to tell my life story—though bits and pieces will help illustrate my points.

Also? I'm human. I'm someone who has fallen and gotten up and fallen again and learned why I was falling—only to find myself falling once more. These 12 principles or steps are about goal setting. They are about understanding who you are and how to bring the idea of abolition to the forefront in your life and in the lives of others. I can't say I always live up to every principle that we need to dismantle white supremacy, but these are the ingredients. My version of the recipe is not always perfect. I get up and try every day.

Why this work?

First, a fact I've come back to, time and again, in my work as an abolitionist: The United States is the world's largest jailer. We need to take that in and really digest it. This country, third in population (dwarfed by China and India), is the largest jailer of humans on the planet. Most recent numbers show the United States at just over two million prisoners. China has 1.7 million prisoners and India has less than half a million—all according to the World Prison Brief.

We also have the most military bases in the world. The United States has bases in more than 70 countries. Many countries have no military bases on foreign soil!

Here is the quickest of history lessons because it's important for context. In both 1899 and 1907, world leaders met in The Hague in the Netherlands to negotiate a series of treaties and to decide what actions would be labeled "war crimes." These meetings became known as the Hague Conventions.

The agreement banned things like:

- Planning a war or an atrocity while under a peace treaty
- Murder or ill-treatment of prisoners of war
- Murder of hostages
- Torture or inhumane treatment
- Destruction of cities, towns and villages
- Devastation not justified

Also, these actions against civilians were banned:

- Murder
- Extermination
- Enslavement
- Deportation
- Mass systematic rape

It was decided that individuals could be held criminally responsible for the actions of a country or its soldiers—although people who win a war are generally not tried for war crimes. (Vietnam is a notable exception, as Americans were tried for war crimes committed there, although the United States is considered the winner of the conflict.)

The list of offenses (it's just a partial one) seems pretty open and shut. Basically, it boils down to *yes, war is hell, but don't be inhumane.*

So, when it comes time to evaluate these war crimes, and many others, which country has committed the most human rights atrocities both during war and peacetime, against others and its own citizens?

The United States of America.

Is it a surprise, with such a militaristic history, that this country has tear-gassed protesters within its own borders? That the United States ships arms and money to territories around the world to support its own need for control? And that those actions have led to harm all over the globe? The Stockholm International Peace

Research Institute reported that the United States was the largest exporter of weapons from 2015 to 2019. Russia, at number two, exported 76 percent less than the United States.

Here's how the United States' approach breaks down with an individual country. According to the US Department of State, since 1978, Egypt has received over $50 billion in military assistance. Giving this kind of aid to countries like Egypt is supposedly intended to open up an ability for the United States to negotiate with them. But in 2013, when Americans pleaded with Egypt to recognize and protect two camps of nonviolent protesters, there was no response. The urgent request from the United States, a country that sends Egypt billions in the name of diplomacy, was simply denied. Nearly 1,000 Egyptian peaceful protesters were killed by the Egyptian military on a single day in August of 2013.

The United States may talk about peacekeeping, but that's never truly been the goal. Just because you don't see the footage of war on social media or the nightly news doesn't mean it's not happening. Our country funds war like it's trying to win a video game. We thrive on conflict, incarceration, crime and punishment, at home and abroad.

All of this is on top of the active genocide of the indigenous people of Turtle Island (their name for North America), a people who lived on this land for thousands of years before it became the United States of America.

There is blood on the hands of this country and the bloody handprints have been left all over the world.

This is where abolition enters.

What Is Abolition?

Abolition: (noun) the action of abolishing a system, practice or institution.

Abolition centers on getting rid of prisons, jails, police, courts and surveillance. Period. How it affects us is so much more than that.

Abolition is a social justice movement. It's my goal with this handbook to make it clear what abolitionist practice looks like in your day-to-day life. No matter what part of social justice is your personal bellwether, the abolition of prisons, jails, police, courts and surveillance must be part of that struggle.

Are you committed to improving education in your city? Does your city use armed police officers in the schools? Abolitionist practice is part of your fight.

Are you concerned with water pollution in your city? Did you know the *Ecologist* has ranked the U.S. military as one of the largest polluters in the world? Abolition is part of your fight.

Are you concerned with mental health care in your community? According to the National Association for Mental Illness, every year, two million people who need access to mental health care end up in jails and prisons instead. Abolitionist practice is part of your fight.

Are you concerned with animal rights? The U.S. government subsidizes both meat and dairy, even at a time when both industries have less and less demand. Instead of letting the people make their own decisions through market value, the government intervenes, even when it's not the healthier alternative. Dairy and beef lobbyists spend billions in our courts and on our politicians to continue their exploitation of animals. Abolitionist practice is part of your fight.

Are you being locked out of the billion-dollar legal marijuana industry? It's by design. There are people sitting in U.S. jails for selling marijuana while others are on the outside making a legal living doing the exact same thing. Abolitionist practice is part of your fight.

Are you a musician using a streaming service? An *in-depth breakdown* from the Manatt, Phelps & Phillips law firm explains that you will receive about 12 cents for every dollar of revenue your work earns. Almost 60 cents goes to your record label, and the rest goes to the streaming service. The U.S. government created this system. If you want to fight for better financial terms, you'll have to go through the court system, and your attorneys will make more than you ever could. If you want to see this changed, abolitionist practice is part of your fight.

If there is any part of your life where you are trying to get free, it connects to abolitionist practice.

Abolitionist practice is also about establishing a system that is rooted in dignity and care for all people. A system that does not rely on punishment as accountability.

What abolitionist practice is *not*: This is not about fixing a broken system. We are not looking for better food or more access to education in prison. We are looking to abolish the entire system.

When people hear the world *abolitionist*, they usually think of slavery. Like the mission to abolish slavery, we don't have a halfway mark. Abolitionists didn't say, let's just make slavery *better*. Let's get them better shoes and dentures and clothing and fewer beatings and better hours on the plantation and the right to marry and keep their babies.

No, the system had to be abolished. As does the prison system, which shares much in common with the system of slavery.

What Does TRANSFORMATION Look Like?

Here's an example. In many states in this country, anything dealing with family "issues" is handled in criminal court. It's unconscionable. If a cis man parent wants to file for visitation with his child, he is *automatically* listed as the defendant in the case. Even if he filed first. The narrative is that no matter what happens, he will need to defend himself. If the courts decide that the father needs to pay child support, it's often handled through the same office that processes cash bails, payouts for lawsuits and other criminal matters.

A father who can't (or won't) keep up with payments can go to jail, lose his passport and be subject to other punitive measures. This doesn't help the child, the mother, the father or the larger community. Punishing someone for not making payments by making them unable to make payments doesn't work and it doesn't get us closer to transforming ourselves and the world.

We need policies that allow for transformation. We need communities to have the opportunity to support their citizens, to create the family structures that work for their people. Is it a council of elders? Is it self-led sessions to work out conflicts?

We need to think this way in order to get free.

Transformation includes a system for all to have access to free health care. Free means you don't have to have a certain job—or marry someone who does—in order to get a certain level of health care.

Transforming ourselves and the world means we have access to the seeds, soils and space to grow our own visons of freedom, resilience and possibility for a different world. Our collective joy, creativity and courage will be our new sustenance. This new world we are working to build will let us live purposeful and fulfilling lives in which we will witness the fruits of our labor in our children, siblings and all those who come after us.

ABOLITION IS:

People's power

Love

Healing justice

Community care

Mutual aid

Transformative justice

Black liberation

Internationalism

Anti-imperialism

The dismantling of structures

Practice, practice, practice

We dare to imagine a world without cages, shackles and chains. As those before us imagined, as well.

Our work, at least for my generation, has a framework that has been laid out for us for years. Professor Angela Y. Davis continues to shape our work and has for decades. Frantz Fanon, Ruth Gilmore and Audre Lorde—these are the people who help us center abolition through many lenses, including a Black, queer and trans feminist lens.

It is often asked if abolition has reparations as part of its goals. Of course it does. Reparations are abolition in action. As noted in my *Harvard Law Review* article on prison abolition:

Abolition calls on us not only to destabilize, deconstruct, and demolish oppressive systems, institutions, and practices, but also to repair histories of harm across the board. Our task is not only to abolish prisons, policing, and militarization, which are wielded in the name of "public safety" and "national security." We must also demand reparations and incorporate reparative justice into our vision for society and community building in the twenty-first century. Reparations campaigns encompass a wide array of demands. Most commonly, reparations in our contemporary movements are justified by the historical pains and damage caused by European settler colonialism and are proposed in the form of demands for financial restitution, land redistribution, political self-determination, culturally relevant education programs, language recuperation, and the right to return.

Let's discuss how we make this happen.

The 12 Steps to Transforming Yourself and the World

1. Courageous Conversations
2. Respond vs. React
3. Nothing Is Fixed
4. Say Yes to Imagination
5. Forgive Actively, Not Passively
6. Allow Yourself to Feel
7. Commit to Not Harming or Abusing Others
8. Practice Accountability
9. Embrace Non-Reformist Reform
10. Build Community
11. Value Interpersonal Relationships
12. Fight the U.S. State Rather Than Make It Stronger

We will discuss each of these principles in the pages that follow. Each principle or step that I explain will be followed by six sections that I think will be helpful:

What to Read/Watch/See/Hear: There are many ways to illustrate each principle here. Sometimes it's a great album, sometimes it's a novel, book, scholarly journal article or podcast. I'll give you some thoughts on how to extend your practice on the topic.

What I Know: I've had many experiences that have informed the principles I try to practice daily. I am continually realizing how the principles ring true for me. For each principle, I'll give you my personal thoughts.

What You Know: I learn from the experiences of others who have shared them with me. It's these everyday experiences that help us see how an abolitionist practice truly works.

Those Who Can, Show: There are stories from those within the movement, those whose stories I know, respect and use as a compass. I'll share these, and I'm sure they'll have the same impact for you.

How We'll Grow: Many of the principles in this book are heavy lifts. I don't expect you to be able to start having courageous conversations or using your imagination after reading a few chapters. I've worked in this social justice movement for over 20 years, and honestly some of these principles are second nature for me. Even so, I have to work on these principles every day. You will, too. I welcome you to explore and grow here.

The Real World: For each principle, I'll share a real-world scenario. I mean, even abolitionists make Target runs sometimes. It's complicated. These sections will encompass what these ideals look and feel like in our day-to-day lives.

To begin our journey, let's start with courageous conversations. This is a fundamental chapter because any part of abolitionist praxis includes meaningful and thoughtful communication. Learning how to communicate with the people you live, work and interact with every day will be critical to your work as an abolitionist.

Let's get courageous.

STEP #1

Courageous Conversations

"Patrisse," my mom said. "I need to talk to you."

From my mom's body language and lack of eye contact, I knew something was up. We didn't do much in the way of dialogue unless it was about day-to-day things. Mom was busy. I slid next to her, holding my breath. My mom, a religious woman who worked hard and did her very best to parent us, was always on the move. She was either at work, on her way to work or just coming home from work. Sometimes, when I saw her, I honestly didn't know which way she was coming or going.

"What's wrong, Mom?" I asked.

"It's about family," my mom said. "Things you need to know."

I felt hairs standing up on my arms and on the back of my neck. My stomach was immediately twisted in knots. Was everyone okay? *Family.* It was something connected to my dad. I could feel it. I didn't know what exactly but I could tell. I had already learned that if I got really upset sometimes, my mom would get upset, too. I was learning from a very early age to not get emotional. I took a deep breath, trying to make sure whatever it was, I could handle it without bursting into tears.

The reason why I was so concerned was that my mom was actually sitting down. She was not making eye contact and not moving. If my mom had to tell me anything, she did it while she was getting dressed or undressed, making dinner, or even talking on the phone with someone. This time she was only talking to me. Someone had to be dead. Mom cleared her throat.

"Your dad is your dad. But not biologically," my mom said, her voice soft but firm.

I did the math in my head. Everyone was alive and well. I now had not one dad but two. My siblings were still my siblings. My mom was still my mom. Patrisse was still Patrisse. I could handle this.

We talked. She explained how we would go about handling this new relationship. I asked some questions, she answered some, brushed off a few. I can honestly say, I knew it was tougher on her than it was on me. I know my mom would have preferred to not have that conversation with me. She also knew she didn't want me to hear that from anyone else. I was already old enough to start to wonder. Certain things weren't adding up.

This was my first introduction to courageous conversations. Sometimes, we have to go to a deep internal space for a conversation. There's honesty, but sometimes you have to go beyond honesty and be courageous. Parents from my mom's generation weren't given the tools for courageous conversations. People could go 30 years not knowing that their sister was actually their mom. Or that they were adopted. Or that their dad wasn't their bio dad. Whether or not she was being pushed to tell me or she just wanted me to know, she broke through and spoke to me. In our religious household, where there was constant talk of sin, Hell and Armageddon, to bring up something that could in any way make her culpable (though not in my eyes) had to take bravery and trust.

Twenty years later, I had to do the same with her.

"Mom, I need to talk to you."

My mother did a double take. She knew I was serious. I saw something in her eyes. It was concern, maybe fear. Maybe both.

She wouldn't always be privy to everything—after all, even though we were living together, I was an adult and a mom myself and had a hectic schedule. But occasionally, she needed to know.

I went to the printer in the office, gathered the papers and sat across from my mom, my heart pounding and my hands nervously flipping through the pages.

"I'm writing a book."

My mom looked me up and down.

"You're writing a—"

"Yes, a book. I'm almost done. It's coming out next year."

"A book about *what*, Patrisse?"

Now, I'm a grown woman and I've been through some things. I'm strong and continually building myself to be even stronger. Let me tell you something, like most women with no-nonsense moms, when my mother

says *Patrisse* in a certain way, it hits my veins like ice water. I needed more than just courage to have this conversation with my mom. I needed several therapy sessions
and some pep talks from my friends. I was not going to
back down from the conversation. But I'm telling you,
I've stood up to a lot of people. I've explained some uncomfortable things to countless people. I've broken up
with people. I've fired people. I've confessed my love. I've
shrunk in fear. Nothing compares to telling your mom
something that you know will displease her.

"The book is called *When They Call You a Terrorist*," I
said. "It's a memoir."

My mom looked at me directly.

"A memoir? That means you're telling your life
story."

I nodded.

". . . And *mine*," she said with emphasis.

I moved around in my seat, trying to find a way to
sit that didn't involve me shrinking into the cushions. I
needed to stay upright, keep my shoulders back, make
eye contact and state my case. I wasn't looking for permission to tell my story. I also wanted her to know I would
respect her and do my best not to embarrass her. What
I had to keep thinking to myself was *my story is mine . . .
my story is mine . . . my story is mine . . . I love my mom but my
story is mine . . .* There's this quote from writer Anne Lamott: "You own everything that happened to you. Tell
your stories. If people wanted you to write warmly about
them, they should have behaved better."

Gulp.

I can't say I quite agree with the quote. My mom did everything she could to be a good mom. Anne Lamott is right in one way though; I own everything that happened to me.

I made eye contact with my mom.

"Of course some parts of your story are part of mine . . ." I started. Then my voice trailed off. I didn't know what else to say.

"I don't think this is a good idea," my mom said. "And I don't want you writing *anything* about me."

Just like that, I was a fidgety, emotional kid again, trying to get my mom to understand something that was important to me. Something I didn't yet have the tools to explain without bursting into tears. Mothers can do that. Even if they want to be understanding. My mom was nervous, mistrustful and angry. Because now I was an adult. She knew I could make these choices if I wanted to. She couldn't send me to my room and say *no writing a book for you!*

When I was still a teenager, I made one of my first radical moves. I started experimenting with my hair. Like most Black moms, my mom wanted my hair manageable and neat, preferably straight. She kept her own hair permed and never went too long without a touchup.

Hair held me back. I wanted to experiment with cuts, color and styles. My mom was firm. Eventually, she had to let go and I had every hairstyle under the sun. Not only did she learn to just let it go, she actually stopped perming her own hair a few years later, which I never would have imagined. Today, she sports a seriously beautiful natural hair look.

I tried to keep that in mind as I had this courageous conversation with my mom. There had been many times that we couldn't see eye to eye on things. Yet every time I approached her with my own will and strength, it turned out well in the end. Maybe not comfortable but always well. I decided that this book could turn out the same.

"Can you tell me what really bothers you about me writing a book?" I asked.

"A lot of things. And I don't think it's necessary for you to do it."

"Is there a way I can help you understand that it's necessary for me?"

"No."

I sighed. Heavily.

"Well, is there a way I can protect you so you don't feel exposed?"

"I don't know. Can you?"

"I think I can."

My mom and I continued to talk about the book and nothing I said made her any more comfortable. She was afraid that she would be represented as a bad mom because of some of the choices she had to make during my childhood. I understood that. I promised her I would be conscious of that *and* that I would let her read any passages directly related to her.

The real work began when I was finishing up the book and dealing with her feelings about some parts of it. It began, like so many things do for an abolitionist, with a courageous conversation.

In order to have a truly courageous conversation, let's break down what the word "courage" means. *Courage,* according to Merriam-Webster, is the mental or moral strength to venture, persevere and withstand danger, fear or difficulty. The word derives from the Middle English word *courage* and from the French *courage,* all the way back to *cor,* the Latin word for heart and also the root word for *core.*

It makes perfect sense that the word "courage" essentially means heart and core because that's where courageous conversations come from—straight from the place where we feel our strongest emotions. We say things like, *it's coming straight from the heart* and *it left me heartbroken.* When we feel emotions like joy, fear and anger, we can often feel our heart beating faster. That's our core. Conversations that begin there are crucial. For some, having an open and honest conversation is just something that *is.* I'm hoping that it will be second nature for my son to have courageous conversations. I and his village are raising him that way.

So why did I, and so many others, have to learn about having courageous conversations? Because courage is a luxury.

Most of my childhood was about survival. Missed meals, governmental neglect of my community, a volatile household run by an overwhelmed, over-worked, underpaid mother—each of these things contributed to my being forced to respond to trauma in ways that no child should ever have to, way before I had the tools, certainly, to manage its psychological effects. Surviving took courage, sure, and I had that. In low-income communities forced to balance on the margins, courage flows like water in the Nile. I was a kid. Soldiering through that trauma rendered me mute—obliterated my ability to be honest about my needs. Indeed, most of the adults in my life, and the children they supported, rarely, if ever, had their needs met. We had the oblique courage to live—but not to speak up.

See, when you grow up poor, you are told often that you don't deserve things—a safe community, access to healthy food, a just justice system, access to social services, a good education. Love. And you believe it. Which means that you give up on making any kind of request for help and understanding—or even thinking you have the right to make one.

I watched my mother work two and three jobs most of my life and rarely asking the people around her—whether family or community—for support, despite desperately needing it.

I have this memory of knocking on her door and, as I leaned in, hearing her muffled crying on the other side. As a grown-up and mother, I see with crystal-clear clarity how doing it alone had to have been breaking her—tearing her into pieces that were too hard and heavy to put back together sans help. Still, there was no one she could talk to—no one she could ask to show up for her in the ways that would have lifted the burden, even just a little bit, for a little while.

That should happen to no one. Honestly, it is a sheer miracle that my mom made it to the other side. I'll never forget what it looked and sounded like to be that vulnerable and bereft. I can only imagine how many courageous conversations my mom tried to have with bill collectors, employers, partners and ex-partners about life-or-death situations.

What's more, the ability to name a need and make a request would have required a vulnerability that we are told equals weakness. The courageous are strong, remember: ours was a community where, no matter what you were going through, the motto was, "You suck it up. You don't ask for help. You do things on your own." Having courageous conversations—the kind that require one to acknowledge neglect's impact, its trauma, and that lead to a request for help—well, that was a no go. I can't help but think how different my mother's journey would have been had she had the skill set, wherewithal, gumption and invitation to name her needs.

Now, that inability to communicate wasn't of her own doing. Racial capitalism—which is inherently patriarchal—impedes our ability to understand just how ingrained this toxic silencing is in our everyday interactions. Many of us, including myself, were taught in homes, places of worship, schools and many other institutions to hold back our words, not necessarily because someone explicitly told us to be secretive but rather because we witnessed all the adults around us who lacked the courage to be honest with themselves and others. This is not a judgment; it is an observation.

We do what we learn, and we practice what is shown to us. As a young, poor, Black girl, I learned that keeping secrets was largely about my survival and safety. For instance, my mom asked us not to be fully honest with state workers because she knew that honesty could jeopardize her ability to continue to be our parent—that if she didn't live up to a particular set of standards, we could be taken away from her.

This is not to be hyperbolic; I witnessed several Black mothers have California's Department of Children and Family Services call on them because a child told a (usually white) social worker that her mother yelled at her. You learned to keep your mouth shut.

That inability to communicate needs passed down to me like blood and nutrients through an umbilical cord, becoming a hindrance in my friendships and dating life. I would bottle everything up inside and when I was completely at my wits' end, I would have terrible outbursts. Healthy communication wasn't an option because I didn't know how to execute that; I had models neither inside my family nor in my community, and so, like any child who soaks up what they learn from their environment, I simply did as the adults did: I struggled, too.

I saw courageous conversations, and I filed them away for moments like telling my mom I was writing a book about my life. I didn't have the phrase "courageous conversations" back then. Nor did I know when I needed to reflect. I stored the conversations just the same.

In high school, it was a scene with my younger sister and my teacher Vitaly that I stored.

I was 17, in twelfth grade. My sister Lynn had come out as queer in middle school. Even though she was younger than me, she was someone I looked up to in many ways. She was fearless (though it came from rage, as fearlessness often does), and she spoke up and out.

One day, I'm walking down the hall and I can hear her voice. I stop and listen. She and Vitaly can't see me. I can tell that Vitaly, who was very chill and laid back, was upset. I admired Vitaly, too. I remember they had rainbow laces in their Chuck Taylors and they were one of the first adults I knew to be fully out of the closet.

"Lynn, I need to speak with you. It's important."

My sister rolled her eyes and grunted. She didn't storm out. She stayed put.

"I need you to look at me," said Vitaly. "I'd like to feel as if you're actually hearing me."

"I hear you," Lynn said, her voice small.

"I'm trying to create a certain culture in this classroom, based on respect and people's needs being met."

I listened closely from the hallway, waiting for Lynn to tear out of the room angling for a fight with someone—anyone. But instead, it was quiet. I peeked inside. Lynn was . . . *listening.*

"I need appropriate behavior, Lynn. I need you to mutually agree that you can do that."

I peeked again, this time sure she was going to get smart and walk out. She stayed. She was open. Then, they said something I never could have imagined.

"Lynn, what are your thoughts? On what I just shared."

What on earth?! Someone was asking my sister for a specific behavior, like, making a plan for it. Then, asking her thoughts?

"I mean, I guess," said Lynn. "I just feel like—"

I walked away, the voices of Lynn and Vitaly reverberating in my head for the rest of the day. I didn't have the words to name that as a courageous conversation, as I do now. I knew even then that their way of communicating with my sister was special and effective. Vitaly was an adult. In our lives, adults spat out commands while hungry, weak and behind the eight ball. Children had to just obey. Period. This was an adult who was courageous enough to look a rage-filled teen straight in the eye—and bring her straight to their core, their combined core. In every sense of that word.

While I never had Vitaly as a teacher, I would visit them often and was witness to the ways they spoke to students—in a way that was so different from the verbally abusive culture that many of the adult figures in high school settings employ. Unlike the other adults, who would scream at us to get to class or punish us for being late, Vitaly spoke to us with love, compassion and care even as they set clear boundaries with students about what was acceptable behavior and what was not going to be tolerated.

I was further exposed to transformational educators when I met Ariane and Susanna, who taught English and interdisciplinary Humanities courses, and were using mindfulness meditation in the classroom as a learning tool. It was this kind of modeling that started to really shape and influence how I wanted to be in conversation with my community. They taught me the importance of grounding, deep listening and being present in conversations.

Understand this, there's preparation for courageous conversation.

It's not something we're born being able to do. For most abolitionists, emerging and beyond, the key components have to be learned.

It was in my late teens and all throughout my twenties that I was able to put the practice into use in movement work. As part of an intentional artist/educator collective called Tribe of the Diasporas, I helped advance the organization's mission to unlearn so many of the toxic practices we had embodied due to racism, sexism, ableism, classism, homophobia and addiction. We accomplished our mission by doing two things: we hosted and invested in developing large-scale public and theatrical artistic events so that we could create spaces for the community to practice authentic engagement, and we met on a monthly basis in a space we named Tribes Day so that we could practice those same principles among ourselves.

From 2005 to 2011, Tribe of the Diasporas hosted monthly events in South Central and Downtown Los Angeles, bringing people together across race, gender and class for events that challenged the misogyny and homophobia that ran rampant in our communities. One of our most successful was thrown in November 2005, when we hosted a large-scale musical event and party in a Downtown Los Angeles warehouse, open to the public, with few restrictions for attendance.

Hundreds of bodies streamed into the open-concept, cement warehouse party. In any other setting, the party would have had a bouncer checking for weapons and drugs to confiscate and for an I.D. for proof that the folks coming to the party were of age. Our bouncer, with his long ponytail, lean but muscular frame and confident stance, was given a different set of instructions; he was to read a script to each person who came to the door.

When entering this party, you are entering with the understanding that there will be no hate speech against queer people, women, Black and Brown people, and trans people. You will respect this space as a sacred space. If you are unable to abide by these guidelines, please turn around and go to another party.

Every individual had to simply verbally consent to follow the guidelines of our party. Just like Vitaly and Lynn in that classroom. This was important because homophobia and transphobia have historically and presently led to violence and death in our communities. We felt an obligation to keep our people safe, but we also saw this as an opportunity to have a cis-het, man of color bouncer both agree with our guidelines and also be the messenger of these femme-led rules. The party wasn't just a place to have fun; it was a way to develop a courageous space that encourages courageous practice.

There was not a single negative event that night. We all trusted and believed in one another and that silent conversation was one of the most courageous of all.

What to Read/Watch/See/Hear: Check out NPR's podcast *Code Switch*. There are often some thoughtful and courageous discussions on race. Episodes like "Is It Time to Say R.I.P. to 'POC'? "and "The Black Table in the Big Tent."

What I Know: I know that courageous conversation will be more than a one-off situation. It's an ongoing process and something you will not always get right. The key for this principle, and many of the ones to come, is to find space for quiet thought. Someone may be spreading misinformation about you (I've been there), a sibling or loved one may be hitting you in a place that hurts (been there, too), or someone in the movement could be criticizing your work (yup, been there, too!). If you can, try silence and peacefulness. Think about what you're feeling. Think about what *that* person might be feeling. What's the end result you want to accomplish? Look, if it doesn't quite work out that way, be gentle with yourself. There will always be another time to try.

What You Know: Consider this example. I worked on a project with Rose, a married mother of two. Like many, she felt stretched thin, that she wasn't managing any of her many roles as well as she could if she had more help—and yearned for some much-needed rest. With her kids in virtual learning, a parent with Covid-19 and a partner who worked 12-hour days, she honestly felt frayed. She also felt like her partner wasn't seeing her. She needed to a have a conversation with her partner.

Except instead of whispering passive-aggressively about needing help while cooking a meal, Rose decided to make an appointment to sit down with her partner. Before they met, she made a list of what she specifically needed from her partner and why. She needed to be alone for at least an hour a day. She needed support with childcare twice a week so that she could catch up on several different projects. She was not going into this conversation saying she needed "self-care." No, her entire family needed better care. For her family, not just for her, things would have to be reconfigured.

Over a quiet dinner, Rose explained all this to her partner. It was a courageous (and thoughtful) conversation that was direct and ultimately successful. Rose's partner was more than amenable to helping construct a new schedule. The courageous conversation led to actual progress.

Months later, courageous conversations still need to happen regularly for Rose and her family. Now, it could be Rose talking to her partner about a cleaning schedule. Her children began to understand the concept and have often initiated their own courageous conversations with their parents and each other.

If you can begin a courageous conversation with a good friend or a partner or your child, it will definitely be helpful as you are working inside of the movement. Attempting to communicate with people you don't necessarily know personally will take intention and skill.

Those Who Can Show: Sometimes, a courageous conversation is one person speaking to millions. It is a call to action and a call for help. The story of Mamie Till Mobley begins with her birth on November 23, 1921, in a small town near Webb, Mississippi. The only child of cotton field workers John and Alma Carthan, Mamie proved to be a bright child who devoted herself to her schoolwork. Early on in Mamie's childhood, the Carthan family moved out of Webb when her father found work in the small industrial town of Argo, Illinois, where Mamie would meet her husband, Louis Till, and welcome her son, Emmett Louis Till, just nine months after their marriage.

Two years later, Louis and Mamie filed for divorce, and Louis was shipped off to Europe as an Army private. Three years later, Mamie received a letter from the Department of Defense that Louis Till was killed due to "willful misconduct." There was no full explanation offered to Mamie or her son Emmett for their tragic loss.

Recent investigations made by writer John Edgar Wideman led him to believe that Louis Till was wrongfully accused, like so many Black soldiers in the segregated Army during World War II, and lynched without a fair trial.

Life continued for Mamie and Emmett, however painfully, in the city of Chicago as she worked more than 12-hour days to provide for her son as a single mother. She recounts how independent Emmett was and how, even at a young age, Emmett took care of the household chores while she was away at work.

Their bond was like no other. In the summer of 1955, Mamie would unknowingly say goodbye to her 14-year-old son for the last time as she sent him alone to visit her family down in Money, Mississippi. On August 31, 1955, the barely recognizable body of Emmett Till was found on the bank of the Tallahatchie River— the only way they were able to identify the body was through a ring with the initials "LT" on his hand, an heirloom left to Emmett from his father, Louis Till. It would take days for Mamie to discover that her only son had been brutally murdered.

Upon the discovery of Emmett's body, Mississippi sheriff Clarence Strider ordered immediate burial "as is" at the local grave site in Money, without the consent of Mamie. The grave was almost finished when Mamie demanded that the body be transported to Chicago so she could confirm the identity and have a proper burial for Emmett. Mamie retells the story of when she first saw the coffin, tightly sealed with three padlocks, and had to sign an affidavit to be able to view the body inside. The undertaker had warned her that the sight might be too gruesome, but nothing could have prepared Mamie for when the coffin was broken open and she saw the remains of her beloved son. It was clear that Emmett's body had been brutally beaten; there was a bullet hole in his head and there were severe abrasions on his neck from the barbed wire his assailants had used to tie his body to a large metal fan, in order to weigh it down in the river.

In various interviews, Mamie, more courageous than many of us will ever have to be, said to reporters, "I have a job to do."

The immeasurable pain she experienced as she endured the vision of her barely recognizable son, whose face had "all the human being battered out of it," compelled her to make the valiant decision to have an open-casket viewing. She wanted the public to see the violence exacted on her son. The open-casket viewing lasted for five days and approximately 100,000 people from all over the country came to pay their respects to Emmett. The image of his body on display made headline news all over the world. Meanwhile, J.

Edgar Hoover (the FBI director at the time of the Till murder) claimed that there were no federal laws that had been violated and therefore he could not take any action on this case.

Mamie refused to stand down and so began to strategize with leaders such as Medgar Evers of the NAACP and Dr. T. R. M. Howard to build a case against the murderers of Emmett Till. Mamie received no support from the justice system and was called a communist, while the suspects—two white men—were provided with five lawyers and had a whole town backing them. In 1955, a year after the Supreme Court ruling in *Brown v. Board of Education*, the South remained deeply segregated, and Mamie describes how on the first day of the trial, the courtroom did not have a space for Black people to sit and so the trial had to be rescheduled to make a table for Mamie and her team of lawyers. Despite this, Black folks lined the walls of the courtroom in support of Mamie. The all-white jury acquitted the defendants, Roy Bryant and J.W. Milam, after 67 minutes of deliberation.

This grotesque miscarriage of justice sparked a worldwide courageous conversation about this country's racism and blatant protection of white supremacists and their violent tactics to repress Black bodies. Mamie bravely took to the streets and joined Civil Rights leaders to give speeches across the nation to confront the judiciary system that was so resolute on protecting and exonerating these acts of hatred fueled by racism. She made it clear that she was not going to be intimidated or silenced and continued to inspire many other women—mothers especially—who were watching the intergenerational impacts that white supremacy and capitalism had on them, their parents and their children.

Mamie called the world to action, and Black people and our allies answered. Emmett Till's death was a powerful and lasting symbol of the segregated South, and Mamie valiantly carried her message of outrage and indignation that would thrust the Civil Rights Movement forward. Emmett's murderers were never held accountable, but Mamie's contribution to social justice ensured that his legacy became his justice. In one of her memorable speeches, Mamie reminds us that we are all we got and we have a responsibility to show up for one another: "The murder of my son has shown me that what happens to any of us, anywhere in the world, had better be the business of us all."

How We'll Grow: To practice courageous conversations, we must first build a foundation for them in our interpersonal relationships. How we communicate with one another impacts the way we move in collectives and within the community. If we live in a community that centers secrets, gossip and rigidity, then we are setting ourselves up for a very toxic environment that is truly antithetical to liberation of self and the people around us. When we are unable to identify harm caused, name our needs and communicate them clearly and directly, our ability to be in authentic relationships with ourselves and others is hindered.

This is to say that when I talk about having courageous conversations, I am largely talking about the conversations you are having inside of intentional community and family building. I do not mean for you to start by having courageous conversations with people with whom you have no foundation.

In fact, the people you want to start practicing with are the ones with whom you want to build for the long term. They are the ones who love and support you. When I'm deciding whether I want to have a courageous conversation with someone, it's often when both the person and I have had a history of being in community and we have shared values and respect and love for one another.

We have courageous conversations because our goal is to live inside of a healthy community that values the dignity of every single human being. We are able to value our lives more if we make the time to engage ourselves and each other with honesty, directness and the courage it takes to speak our truths.

A slight in the supermarket does not (necessarily) call for a courageous conversation. A long-unhealed scar with a sibling or a loved one does.

When you are preparing for a courageous conversation, it's important you identify the intentions behind the conversation. What are your personal goals and what exactly are you asking of the individuals? Do you have concrete requests? Do you want an apology? Do you want changed behavior? Ask yourself as many questions as possible so that you are clear on your intent, your asks, and your expectations. I would encourage you to write it all down so when you do communicate with your community member, you have notes to reference. Remember this: the person doesn't owe you anything. Just because you've asked and you want to have a courageous conversation, this person doesn't have to apologize, grant your requests or be in conversation with you. Your goal is to come from the right place. You can't create expectations for the other person.

Anyone can initiate a courageous conversation, but I think the moment you sense or feel discomfort toward another person is a good time to communicate with them transparently about what is coming up for you. Otherwise, this practice can backfire badly.

Once you've mastered this (and don't be surprised if it takes some time, I'm still working on it), then take the practice outside of your home and into the community—*your* community. Find a good practice partner—someone who is mutually invested in co-creating a healthy relationship, is invested in their own healing journey, and is able to value and practice shared responsibility.

The Real World: Here's the real deal that some in my position might not say. Movement work isn't always sweet. There is conflict. Activists, even those who are doing their very best for their communities, can and will beef. There are people in movement work that I'm not particularly friendly with. Don't necessarily need to grab a cup of coffee on a weekend. We can be cordial and we can definitely fight together for getting free. It's liberation, nothing personal. Remember that historically, movements have lost their way due to external and internal forces and conflict. Think about how courageous conversations can prevent those narratives from affecting the dynamic of your organizations.

GUIDING QUESTIONS

1. Are you capable of having a courageous conversation? Why or why not?
2. When was the last time you had one? What happened? How did you grow?
3. If you had to have a courageous conversation, who would you have it with (outside of a friend or family)? What is the outcome you're looking for in having that courageous conversation? Who will benefit? How will it benefit the greater good?
4. How will your courageous conversation move you closer in your abolitionist practice?

Respond vs. React

"Patrisse. We're not going to St. Louis."

I stuffed my suitcase and clicked the lock.

"What are you talking about?"

I was six months pregnant and trying to make sure that I wasn't jeopardizing my health or that of my baby. I still had energy and space to work. If we were needed, we were there. Looking back, I realize I was moving on fumes. I was also committed. If I was expected somewhere—I was going.

"If we go, there's a group of people that are threatening to end the event and also—"

My friend looked away.

"And also what?"

"People are saying they're trying to fuck us up, Patrisse. For real."

I sighed. And unlocked my luggage.

Movement work often means travel is imminent. I'm getting used to it, but it still takes a lot out of you to stay on the road and in the air. Sometimes, things go down and we have no choice but to suit up and head out.

So, several years ago, I and my team and co-leaders were ready to go. Our flights from Los Angeles to St.

Louis were booked and we had our itinerary laid out. It was 2015. A year after Mike Brown was murdered. He had been shot and killed by Ferguson police officer Darren Wilson and the community had been protesting ever since. They were exhausted and traumatized.

The co-founders of BLM had been traveling to and from St. Louis to support folks on the ground. We spent months in St. Louis and hours working directly with the young Black women who led the protests outside of the Ferguson police precinct. When we weren't in St. Louis we followed the community response closely. We had heard some rumblings that folks were not feeling BLM, but we did not realize that people were actively talking shit about us. Mike Brown had been shot and killed and left in the middle of the street for four and a half hours. His death led to the protests. It started with a makeshift memorial that was created on the spot where he died. Things were touched off when, allegedly, a police officer urinated on the memorial and later crushed it while driving a police vehicle.

There were two types of protest and civil unrest that were taking place in Ferguson each day. There were news cameras in a media tent in the mornings and afternoons. In the evening, it was a younger, more restless crowd. There were several instances of unrest and stores were burned. There was also healing, with groups gathering to mourn the young man while also fighting to make sure it never happened again.

We talked about if we should be on the front lines

for the protest or playing a different role. The University of Missouri–Columbia invited us to speak about Black Lives Matter. I was excited about going because I had developed really strong relationships with folks on the ground in St. Louis.

Going into a city with unrest is not something I or anyone I build with takes lightly. Because BLM has an international platform, we bring visibility. Which is not always a good thing. Beyond just physical visibility, with the advent of social media, we've seen movements use Instagram, Twitter and Facebook to call out elected officials, racist white folks who call the cops on Black people and corporations who've been outwardly problematic in the face of a more progressive public. What happens when we start using these strategic tactics on each other? Inside of our movements and with our community members? The onslaught of reactivity toward already vulnerable communities has been incredibly dangerous and frankly counterproductive.

The case in St. Louis was during one of Black Lives Matter's most visible moments, and many of us inside the Black Lives Matter leadership were under attack by our national government and by local governments. We faced daily death threats and doxxing.

Still, when my BLM co-founders, Alicia and Opal, and I committed to speaking at the university, we had no idea that people on the ground would want to shut us down. The idea that folks would want to physically harm us? For coming to an event and speaking on behalf of BLM? We were on the same team!

This wasn't the first time or the last time folks inside our movement would talk about us as if we were the elected officials or corporations we spent time challenging publicly. While I agree with the tactic of publicly "shaming" elected officials, white racists and corporations, as a trained organizer you use public shaming as a final tactic once you've tried everything else. Instead of jumping to public shaming, your approach could look like an outreach letter, then one-on-one face time to make specific demands, and then analysis to see if the entity has made any changes. If they have not you go back and remind them of the demands made. If after all of this the entity is continuing to cause harm, you challenge them publicly so that the public at large can hold them accountable.

This doesn't mean we don't ever call visible leaders out publicly, but rather it means we need to and must commit to grounded responses vs. reactionary vitriol. Unfortunately, much of what those in social justice movements have expressed via social media toward movement leaders, activists and folks in friend circles and collectives has been to call for blood instead of accountability. Too often we have been taught that our big emotions justify hurtful and sharp responses.

If you turn on the television and watch any TV show, scripted or unscripted, the characters rarely respond in a grounded way. There is often praise of reactivity, on reality TV shows especially. How many times have you watched *Love & Hip Hop* or *The Real Housewives* and someone throws a drink at someone or humiliates them in front of their community? Very seldom do we see a mature and healthy conversation between two individuals, let alone between two groups of people.

We know that mostly these are not real relationships and that TV is a thinly veiled "reality," which makes this even worse. Many people on these shows are following scripts with this behavior.

The reality is, our goal to speak from a grounded place is incredibly challenging. It means we need to and must look at our own feelings and reactions first. We have to identify what we are truly upset about. We have to assess what kind of community we are trying to build inside of a state that consistently pits us against each other. A grounded response provides a new tool for us as we develop an abolitionist culture.

When hearing that our own people didn't want our help—and further wanted to hurt us instead—I could react or I could respond.

React comes from the Latin verb *reagere*, which means *to do something again*. Makes perfect sense, because often, when you react, you simply act without thinking it through. Meanwhile, to respond is to reply, not necessarily to act. We think before we respond. We sometimes do not think before we react.

Reacting and responding can get the same results,

sometimes. But it's not likely. The effort you put into reacting can end up harming you and your goals.

I don't know why the organizers on the ground in St. Louis reacted the way they did. It wasn't helpful to anyone. If there was anything that concerned them about national BLM leadership, our ears were (and still are) open. Social media threats are reactions. If they had wanted to *respond*, we could have engaged.

We didn't go to St. Louis. It bothered me then and it bothers me now. I have to respond rather than react, as well.

I'm not always on point.

A few years ago, my team sat around a conference room table and mapped out strategy for an upcoming project. We were all exhausted and on edge but trying to hold on and get work done. At one point, someone I'll call Anna called me out for something I did that impacted her.

To react would mean: I would be hurtful and curse her out and tell her she was wrong.

To respond would mean: I would listen and marinate. I would take a minute—or more—to figure out what I wanted to say.

Did I mention that I am *not* always on point?

I yelled at Anna. I reacted, big-time. I left the meeting abruptly, in tears. The meeting continued, but now with the heaviness of reacting rather than responding.

The work of abolition is hard enough on our bodies

and our minds—there is no need to make it more difficult by reacting rather than responding, especially with
our fellow abolitionists. Abolition is about getting free.
Reacting abruptly is not freedom. For you or anyone
else.

This is not new. The idea that some of the people on
the ground in St. Louis did not want BLM leadership
shouldn't seem foreign. We can want the same things—
freedom and abolition—and still not have the same
ideals. We have to respect each other. We don't have to
agree.

In his autobiography, Malcolm X discussed the
March on Washington in 1963. "I was there," he says. "I
observed that circus."

Malcolm made it clear that holding hands with white
allies and singing Negro spirituals like "We Shall Overcome" was not the way to abolition. In *The Autobiography
of Malcolm X*, he barely reined in his disgust for the
march. Malcolm's words were coarse—and honest.

Who ever heard of angry revolutionists all harmo-
nizing "We Shall Overcome . . . Suum Day . . ." while
tripping and swaying along arm-in-arm with the
very people they were supposed to be angrily revolt-
ing against? Who ever heard of angry revolutionists
swinging their bare feet together with their oppres-
sor in lily-pad park pools, with gospels and guitars
and "I Have A Dream" speeches?

We know that Malcolm's and Martin's ideologies could not have been more different from day one until King passed. They were cordial (so we've been told), they met exactly one time, for a photo op, and that was that.

Here's what Malcolm did *not* do. He didn't bum rush the march and try to take over. He didn't march through security and cause a commotion. He didn't interrupt the speeches. He watched, largely in annoyance. At the same time, he understood that King and his followers would act in accordance with their own ideology. He didn't *react* to the march. He *responded*.

We, all of us in movement life, will not always see eye to eye. Sometimes, we'll actually feel like enemies. Sometimes, we'll feel like the people who should be closer to our side are actually closer to the side of our enemies.

Sometimes, and this is perhaps most difficult of all to parse, the people in your *own* organization have to be responded to—rather than reacted to.

In September of 2020, I appeared on the cover of *TIME* with my fellow BLM co-founders Alicia Garza and Opal Tometi as part of the *TIME* 100 list. As we prepared for the shoot, I realized that it was a great honor. More importantly, it was a way to make sure BLM would remain in the forefront of critical conversations.

A week before the shoot I got a phone call from Leslie, one of our people on the ground in a major city.

Leslie had worked her butt off to push the BLM mission both on the streets and in the political process.

After a brief conversation, I asked her if she was calling me for a particular reason. I let her know that I was really proud of the work her crew had done in the past few months. She thanked me. There was something about her voice that threw me off.

"Is everything okay?" I asked.

"Yes," said Leslie. "It's just—"

"Tell me."

"We know that BLM is not about getting press—"

"I know," I said. "But we also know it can be necessary."

"*TIME* magazine called us about being part of the *TIME* 100," said Leslie. "They've been following our mission and were impressed with what we've accomplished."

"That's amazing, Leslie!" I said. "Are you doing a shoot?"

"No," said Leslie, her voice flat. "We turned them down."

"Why?"

"There have been so many other folks who feel like we're getting too much attention."

"For all the right reasons," I said.

"It doesn't matter. If we're on that list, we'll just be a distraction. I don't want to make people feel like we're getting something we don't deserve."

As I think about that conversation with Leslie right

now, my throat tightens up. Those who work as hard as she and her team do every single day, not feeling like they could stand up and be recognized makes me sick. I go through the same thing every day; someone always has something to say about how I am being portrayed. That's what I signed up for. Part of the job these days is representing BLM. Leslie deserves to have her work recognized.

Do I react to this? Or do I respond?

I could've reacted. I could've pushed Leslie to accept the honor from *TIME* and push back against those who had something to say about it. I could have reached out to anyone who had something to say. That would not make her work any easier. Or mine.

I had to take my time, be true to my own feelings, and respond to Leslie. I had to let her know that I would support her no matter what. I had to let her know that I respected her decision, was proud of the work she and her team had done. Then I had to let it go. It didn't feel good to respond when I wanted to react. Sometimes, in this work, it is part of your mental health practice to respond and move on.

Listen, I work with a team of people who work hard. Across the country, there are so many others who are putting their lives and health on the line for this work. Even so, when we feel ramped up, we have to consider our mental health.

The idea of mental health goals and how to take proper care of yourself will come up often in this handbook. Being committed to social justice in all forms means that you will sometimes have to respond rather than react on a daily basis.

I am privileged to live among a community of people who are either directly engaged in my work or supportive and accepting in some way. You may work toward social justice at work but at home deal with people who don't respect your views. Or you may have a strong dynamic at home, made of people who have the same goals you do. But every day, from nine to five, you have to work with people you don't respect but can't react to because you have bills to pay.

You will often want to react to people, ideas, thoughts, media bites, all of it. It will do nothing but make you unnecessarily vulnerable. Which will make your practice much more difficult to hold up. Try your best to separate the wheat from the chaff. Determine what is worth your energy and what is not.

We know that the feelings that come from strong reactions can affect our health, particularly our hearts. How you choose to deal with stressful conversations can literally affect how you practice abolition. Try to remember that keeping calm whenever possible is key. Even when you feel like you can't, try harder. This is a space, among many we'll discuss, where therapy may be helpful to sort these feelings and develop coping mechanisms. If you're not your best self, you're not the best abolitionist you can be, either. This movement needs us to take every moment as it is—not how we want it to be.

(It *still* bothers me that Leslie and her team were not a part of the *TIME* 100. They earned it. I know they are appreciated and will be recognized moving forward. I still have to make sure I remain responsive and not reactive.)

Another thought. An amazing example of responding in the face of white supremacy. Writer Toni Morrison did an interview with a journalist in 1998. The interviewer asked Morrison if she would ever incorporate white lives into her work.

"I have done that," Morrison responded.

"Substantially," the interviewer pushed.

Watching it now, it is almost hard to believe. Morrison had won the Nobel Prize for literature five years earlier. She had won the Pulitzer Prize a few years before that. This white interviewer wanted to know when she was going to write more about white people? It was unconscionable. Morrison would have had every right to curse that woman out and read her for filth.

She did not react. She responded. With grace.

"You can't understand how powerfully racist that question is," said Morrison, her voice barely above a whisper. "You would never ask a white writer why they didn't write about Black people. . . . It's inconceivable that where I already am *is* the mainstream."

Morrison was barely miffed. At least not on the outside. She responded to the journalist. She remained in conversation with the person, and 30 years later, it's still a master class in communication.

It's an art. I can't say I've mastered it. It's worth work-ing on it.

I'm literally still working on it on a day-to-day basis. Just two weeks ago, my mom left me a voicemail that upset me. The story is long and doesn't really matter. Suffice to say, I thought she was being disrespectful and not supportive of me. I went straight to her house, walked right in—and we had a screaming match. I was really hurt and I was really upset.

Listen to me when I tell you, it was *not* a courageous conversation. I was definitely reacting, not responding. I didn't even give it any wait time. I went from listening to the voicemail to arguing with no time in between.

If I could do it over? Honestly, I'm not going to say that every time you don't get it right, you owe someone an apology. To be frank, I stand by what I said to my mom. I did apologize to her, and asking her for a cou-rageous conversation would have been a better plan. However, that didn't happen. It won't always happen. That's okay, too. Sometimes, you have to apologize to yourself for not reacting a certain way.

My final thought on reacting vs. responding. The following situation is something I've spoken about in several presentations and articles, and it never fails to center me when I think of how it was handled. It still guides me as well as pains me.

Ten years ago, I worked with students in a local high school and my position wasn't sharply defined. I was young enough for them to speak freely with me, but I was old enough for them to see me as someone in a position of authority.

It didn't take long for the students to begin to depend on me. We talked about their hopes and dreams, the expectations from their parents, questions about the future.

Miss Patrisse, do I have to go to college?

Miss Patrisse, do you have a boyfriend? Well, do you have a girlfriend?

Miss Patrisse, you're a grown-up now so tell the truth. Do we really need math?

I usually kept the answers short but clear, letting them know I'd always be honest and yet still have boundaries. (For those questions, the answers were *no, both, yes.*) There was a convivial spirit in our spaces, like with Vitaly and my sister Lynn. If you were in conversation with me, you felt respected—and I did, too.

In addition to mentoring the students, I was mentored by older teachers, as well. Throughout my schooling, I was fortunate to have come across many amazing teachers who helped me grow and showed me what justice could and would be like when entrusted to me and my generation. One of those teachers was someone I'll call Mr. Harold. I modeled who I was as a counselor after who Mr. Harold was to me as a teacher. He was firm while still being friendly and accessible. He gave us space to be kids but treated us—and taught us—the same way he would a roomful of adults. I hardly left his class without something to marinate on. As a mentor, a few years later, it was the same. He spoke about pedagogy without making it feel stuffy. He gave me real-world examples of how to connect with my students the way he connected with me. I wanted to be a shining example for Mr. Harold.

I really liked my job as a counselor. It was one of those situations where you looked forward to work every day, and with my young, fresh-faced idealism, I knew I could take over the world—and take those young people with me.

A few months into a new school year, a young woman I'll call Maria asked me if she could speak to me privately. Maria was quiet but worked super hard. She didn't ask as many questions as her classmates. I noticed she listened to them all, sometimes smiling at my answers. So I was surprised that she wanted to speak with me.

"Are you okay, Maria?" I asked.

Maria shook her head *no*, back and forth.

"This is important, isn't it?" I asked.

She nodded her head *yes*. "At least, *I* think it's important. Some people say I'm being silly."

"I won't think that," I said. "What is it?"

"It's about Mr. Harold."

When a student starts off using a teacher's name that way, it's almost never a good look. I felt a little queasy, but I kept a neutral face.

"Miss Patrisse, he's really inappropriate."

Again, stomach drops. I nod my head and gesture

for her to continue. All I could think was *I have to keep her safe. I have to respond not react. No matter what.*

"I was with my friend, Jesi. We saw Mr. Harold and he was, like, super flirty with her. Later on Jesi told me that Mr. Harold and her had sex at a hotel room. I'm really scared. This is not okay."

"I'm glad you could talk to me," I said. "That's courageous and I appreciate it."

"You're not going to tell anyone, are you?"

I exhaled and closed my eyes. "Maria, remember what a mandatory reporter is?"

"Oh. Right. You have to tell someone if you think or know a child is being abused."

I nodded. "I have to tell the authorities about this. We have to keep Jesi safe. But you and I will figure out how to handle this first. So you feel safe, too."

Maria nodded and flicked a tear from her eye. "So, what do we do?" she asked.

Maria and I sat down and talked it out. We looked at what could happen after reporting Mr. Harold. We looked at options on how we could make her safe. She knew that I was equally concerned. Although I hadn't mentioned it explicitly, she knew Mr. Harold was my former teacher. I think she felt safer talking to me about it because she knew I would understand how disconcerting it was.

Talk about a courageous conversation. It still stands out in my mind how courageous Maria had to be and how proud I am that I created a space for her to feel comfortable protecting her friends and herself—and *me.*

Legally, I had to react. I reported the case to the Department of Children and Human Services. As soon as the case was filed, I found out it wasn't the first time Mr. Harold had been reported. There were numerous allegations of sexual misconduct with students.

Here's the part where abolition and courageous conversations get real dicey. I knew I needed to report Mr. Harold and I did so with no hesitation. I was concerned about what would happen next. In the world I was being raised in, as an organizer, there was healing for all. Yes, that included Mr. Harold. In my world, he would not be thrown in jail. This is *not* to say he would not have accountability or not have to make amends for his actions. This means, in my world, we would handle this without police or government intervention. But I had already started that process by reporting what I heard. All I could do was try my best to cause no harm. I asked people in my community for help in supporting Maria, and I stayed in close contact so she could tell me what she needed, as well.

Something else I did, in the name of abolition and courageous conversations and responding vs. reacting: I reached out to Mr. Harold. I told him that I was the one who had reported him. There was no need for anonymity. This was our community and I was going to protect it. I left him a message and let him know that if he wanted to talk about it, we could.

I never heard from him.

Not hearing from Mr. Harold affected me. Perhaps, in some corner of my mind, I thought he would reach out to me and tell me it was a misunderstanding and he hadn't done anything wrong.

I started thinking of all the times I'd been with him, nothing but trusting. It made me feel awful. Then, I thought about the process I'd had to go through. Why didn't we have a system where, perhaps, an elder could approach Mr. Harold? Someone trained in these situations. I had no other option but calling on the state. Would anyone harmed in this scenario be healed? Maria was harmed. Her friend was harmed. I had no way to process my role in any of it.

During that time I signed up to go to a three-day transformative justice training with generationFIVE, an organization dedicated to ending child sexual abuse within five generations. Maria and I traveled together to learn about transformative justice processes and new ways of holding our communities accountable for harm. During that training, I was provided a new language to process what my experience had been as both a former student of Mr. Harold and a mandated reporter and colleague who was obligated to call the appropriate authorities on him.

When Maria and I left the training we went back home and created transformative justice circles for some of the staff of the high school and also some of the students. I never did hear back from Mr. Harold, but I did learn that transformative justice practice can happen even if the person who caused harm isn't willing to be part of the process.

It was important to me that I talk to my peer group about our educational environment. I began to learn that other people I had known were also survivors of sexual abuse at the hands of teachers I had adored. I began learning about CSA (child sexual abuse) through a transformative justice lens. I realized that so much of my abolition work also must apply to this particularly painful issue. I sit here today understanding deeply that our current structures of punishment do not get us closer to ending CSA, and I also sit here understanding that survivors need closure, need healing. My high school caused harm, and in order for that harm to be healed it must first be addressed. And when we address it from a place of response vs. reactivity we create more healing and transformation for everyone involved.

Courageous conversations and learning how to respond and not react got me through. I knew after that incident that it had to be different. There had to be another way to protect. Why couldn't justice also transform?

What to Read/Watch/See/Hear: As a 22-year-old youth counselor, I called on many people to help me remain mindful. It's a practice I was introduced to early on in my schooling and I've always tried to maintain it. It's an invaluable skill to be able to take a breath and then another, then many more. There are many books, podcasts and apps available that will help you with the mindful meditation needed for courageous conversation. Check out Chani Nicholas's new app CHANI, a comprehensive astrology app that can help deepen your courage practice. Thich Nhat Hanh was a teacher of mine, and while he has passed, he has a myriad of books on mindfulness meditation.

What I Know: I know that I feel my feelings deeply (more on that later). So it's important for me to have a default peaceful setting. That means sometimes I have to say *no* to something important in order to say *yes* to myself. Recently, I got a call about an interview I'd been asked to do. It was last-minute, but I really wanted to do it. I looked at my calendar. I would have to miss my therapy appointment in order to do the interview. I thought about canceling my appointment. Surely I'd be able to go another time. I knew what that meant. The next day, I'd get busy and likely not schedule my appointment. The peace that comes with my therapy is critical. I turned down the interview and kept my therapy appointment. I had to process the guilt I felt about not doing it. In order to respond and not react, I had to maintain my peace.

What You Know: In the last chapter, I talked about Rose, who had to have a courageous conversation with her partner about needing help with parenting responsibilities and the household and having time and space for her work. The courageous conversation went well but it started with a lot of reacting instead of responding.

Example: Her partner would be on a last-minute Zoom call for work and unable to put the kids to bed as planned. She would go silent. Giving off irritated vibes, even to the children. After her partner was off the call, she would remain silent. Although they both knew exactly why she was being passive-aggressive, it wouldn't be discussed. Even though she wouldn't make a sound, it was still a reaction instead of a response. She would continue this behavior, which wouldn't open up lines of communication. It would just fill the house with reactionary vibes that wouldn't move things forward and would only make everyone else tense. We all know, at our core, that reactionary responses only worsen our interpersonal relationships. It's easy to remember how to do this in the moment: React has the word "act" in it. That's not what you want to do in any stressful moment. You want to try to prevent yourself from acting. So, try to respond instead.

Those Who Can Show: Phillip Agnew was born in Chicago, Illinois, the son of a preacher and a teacher, and grew up in a home where his father's South Side sermons and mother's gospel ingrained a great love for music as an agent to inspire and unite people. He kept this love close to his heart as he began his career in community organizing as a student at Florida A&M, where he co-founded Dream Defenders as a response to the murder of Trayvon Martin in 2012.

One year later, after Trayvon's killer, George Zimmerman, was acquitted, Agnew spearheaded the Dream Defenders into action as they occupied the Florida State Capitol for 30 nights and 31 days to demand that the Stand Your Ground law be repealed, effective immediately. While the action was not successful in changing the law, it was a catalyst for the mostly Black Floridian youth protesters, who were fighting not just to change one law but to completely transform their communities for the long haul.

Agnew proved to be a powerful youth voice in the nation and was invited to the fiftieth anniversary of the March on Washington to speak to tens of thousands of people on the Lincoln Memorial steps. Agnew was slated to speak among other activists and politicians but was (without notice) cut off the speakers list due to lack of time.

He tried to negotiate his time—he only needed two minutes to deliver his message. Still, his slot was given to a more recognized elder leader in the movement and Agnew was booted off the program.

In this day and age of social media and its indeterminate etiquette, many of us would have reacted and taken the route of calling out this offense and letting the public deliberate on how to make things right. He could have tweeted out heavy criticism of the elders, tagging the right people to get the incident written up. He could have written a piece outlining how he was wronged and why he was upset about it. He could have brooded about it and brought it up in interviews and among his organizing communities. Honestly, I would have understood if he reacted that way. It's one thing for me to write *don't react* in a book. It's another to keep that same energy in real life.

Organizers are rightfully wary of the spotlight. But many of us need to speak to our audience—and do it well. Of course, there's some amount of pride there, whether we want to admit it or not. Agnew wrote down his thoughts, rehearsed them and prepped for a good amount of time before the event. Being cut was not just an inconvenience. It likely hurt. Especially as younger organizers often feel like they need to be legitimized and validated by their elders in a way that's complicated and nuanced.

Agnew did something creative—he responded, thoughtfully. He decided that the two minutes on that stage did not actually belong to him. The whole reason he was going up on those historic steps was to amplify the voices of the thousands of young people who were making the oath to join the movement for justice and to reassure the elders that young people were in fact present and ready to take it from here.

So, Agnew made a call to the nation to post a two-minute video of their own with #OurMarch: "Our time was cut from the March [On Washington], but I believe we still have much to say. They told me that they had run out of time, but I believe that our time is now . . . What do you believe? . . . Record your two minutes!

What would you say?" This call to action was heard all over the nation and not only galvanized thousands of youth but also inspired something unexpected: an intergenerational conversation. What was meant to be a microphone for the youth became an honest reflection about ageism within our movement spaces and how we work together to transform those toxic dynamics in real time. Ideas about the politics of respectability, challenging tradition and assumed righteousness were brought to the forefront with #OurMarch in service of building the kind of just world we envision.

Agnew has continued to push the bounds of traditional community organizing through his efforts to center the importance of culture in movement building. In the three years after he started Dream Defenders and led other organizing efforts, he had seen many of his comrades succumb to burnout, isolation and despair. They were overwhelmed with survival—with the constant death and violence enacted on Black people and communities of color making headlines every day—and Agnew devised a way to create a space where the soul could find solace.

In 2016, Agnew and his partner, artist Aja Monet, co-founded Miami's Smoke Signals Studio—a community-based radical artistic space committed to uplifting joy, connection and purpose as integral to the liberation movement. "Our work is in line with cultural organizers that understood to use art is to animate a radical future" and to move people when facts and data are not enough. He attributes his understanding of art as integral to organizing to his partner Aja, a poet, who challenged him to cultivate spaces where art is not simply an accessory to organizing but a means to elevate how we fight to get free.

Agnew's commitment to thoughtful responsiveness continued as he transitioned out of Dream Defenders in 2018 to make space for Black women leaders inside not just the organization but inside the larger movement, as well. He responded to a moment of opportunity, as men are being challenged to cut ties with patriarchy, to honor the women around him whose labor has gone unrecognized and undervalued. While many Black men have reacted to #MeToo and other feminist campaigns by continuing to uphold patriarchy, the more convenient and complacent path, Agnew has relied on something wholly different.

His latest project, Black Men Build, propagates his belief that Black men deserve to be organized into a feminist framework that doesn't deny Black men their dignity but calls them in as a group of people who must see this current struggle as something they should and need to be a part of. He leans into Black men's existing resourcefulness and will to survive and meets them at the intersection of transformation, where he urges Black men to heal the pain of survival and internalized oppression. Black Men Build clearly outlines that this first begins with Black men being held accountable to the hurt and pain they have inflicted on Black women.

This radical approach is yet another example of how Agnew continues to be a leader in deep responsiveness who is training and shaping a whole new generation of Black men who are building a powerful Black future. Black men who are leaning into abolition.

Courageous conversations are the foundation of the response vs. reaction principle. In the earlier example I gave, when we three co-founders were being verbally attacked by Ferguson protesters, we collectively decided we wouldn't travel to St. Louis and we canceled the event at the University of Missouri. This left the student body, the administration and the community at large disappointed. While I believe that canceling the event was our best option, I do believe if we had been practicing the first two abolitionist principles, we may have had a different outcome. More importantly, I believe that our work as human beings must be the prioritization of modeling best practices—practices that will help us root out the ways we are taught to punish people as a reaction to our own hurt feelings or maybe even as a reaction to real and true harm.

Conflict should actually strengthen relationships and community dynamics. We don't have to approach conflict as automatically volatile. We can see conflict the way we understand friction. If you are rubbing two twigs together, eventually the friction can create heat and that heat can turn into fire. If you are not careful with the fire, you can burn yourself, but if you are careful with the fire, the heat can nourish you.

Our practice toward grounded responsiveness offers a model for both our personal relationships and our movement relationships. We can choose to center our values over our reactive vitriol. We can choose to be in community and model a new approach toward naming requests.

Whenever I am in conflict with another person in my life—especially if that person is a movement comrade—I choose to be in conversation with that person. The moment I feel impacted by someone I check in with myself to be clear what feelings are coming up for me. Am I hurt by the thing this person did or what they represent to me in my life? Can I have a conversation with this person to practice a new way of being in relationship with them?

I choose to communicate with the person who I feel has harmed or hurt me no matter how small or big the issue is. My grounded response reflects my belief that we must have a bigger vision for our communities and the people who make up our communities. Unless you are a troll, I don't block a community member from social media.

I believe in coming back into the community and trusting that modeling grounded responses vs. reactive vitriol will allow for an opening inside of the relationship that is then modeled inside of the larger movement community. Or, at the very least, that will keep me from losing my cool and help me keep my own levels balanced.

Abolition must be a cultural intervention. It must

produce a new way of being even in the most challenging and difficult moments. We have not collectively practiced abolition, so it's hard for us to understand its significance. If we implement a new practice that is centered in care and dignity, we might find a practice that challenges our instinct to "cancel" each other. Abolition is about how we treat each other. It is about how we show up in relationships. Abolition is about how we respond to harm caused and how we respond when we cause harm.

I don't believe abolition is about bullying, but I do believe abolition is about standing up for yourself. We need to be committed to building a culture that is rooted in care, dignity and accountability. Let's never forget the consequences of a draconian and antiquated system.

How We'll Grow: If you're in a meeting, perhaps about movement work, get used to keeping a notebook and pen nearby. Sometimes, we dive into reacting when we really need to absorb what's being said. If you hear something that doesn't sit well with you, write it simple and clear: *I don't like the idea Nicole is suggesting and it's making me uncomfortable* or *I don't feel like my ideas are being heard and it's making me angry. I don't like X and it's making me feel Y.* Taking it out of your head and resting it somewhere else may not end the discomfort, but you can at least temporarily subdue it instead of ramping up the emotion.

Some people who don't want to write these things

down can just take a break, leave the area (or put the call on hold), and create a voice memo, getting out the thoughts quickly before returning. Later, you can write them down. This early exercise serves two purposes. You can slow down your reaction time, and later the voice memos or notes can be a part of the conversation if the issue must be addressed. You can say to your comrade, *I wrote this note when I was in react mode. Can we talk about it?*

The idea that you can share with someone how you felt *before* you respond is valuable and will undoubtedly help the person respect your thoughts, even if it doesn't change their mind.

Keep these first efforts very small and make sure they are about small things before you find yourself in larger conflicts. (Yes, there will be larger conflicts. It's just the way these things go.)

This, like all things you will consider as you grow in your abolitionist practice, will take time, practice and energy.

This is an ongoing journey. At some point you will find it easier and easier to stop and take a beat before reacting. You'll have moments where you'll find yourself backsliding. Any number of things may trigger an inability to handle your thoughts and feelings. It could be physical illness, a mental health crisis, anxiety—just be prepared.

Below, some thoughts on how to move forward with this practice. Keep in mind, you can also use these as an exercise in hypothetical scenarios with those you live and work with. Check out the guiding questions at the end of this chapter.

The Real World: The Notorious B.I.G. said it best: "Mo Money, Mo Problems." Money is a sticky and thorny discussion in any industry. It can build and destroy any organization. Even an anti-capitalist organization will still have to deal with the money—sometimes quite a bit of it—that fuels that same system. Because most activism begins in a grassroots scenario, it can be disconcerting when donations begin to come in and the organization becomes well known. How do you make sure you don't become the very thing that you are fighting against?

Many organizations that I have developed and worked for have been criticized for how they spend their money. There will always be some tension between volunteers who work very hard and salaried full-time employees who do the same. All you can do is make sure the team is tight, honest and follows all the rules both internally and externally. Be as transparent as possible—but make no apologies for salaries and other expenses.

Everything I represent is all about criticizing organizations, even ones like my own. Since I know what it's like to call a group to task, I know I need to be prepared for it myself.

Example: There was a dustup surrounding BLM using an organization called ActBlue to assist with managing donations. Like crowd-funding or PayPal or any other processor, ActBlue takes a small amount of the donation in order to process the funds so that organizations don't have to spend so much money on accountants and staffers to manage fundraising. Many progressive organizations, including Joe Biden's team, have used ActBlue. There's a similar organization called WinRed that often works with Republican candidates.

Because ActBlue works with Democratic organizations and some candidates, the story became that BLM was just a shell and all of the money was going straight to the Democratic Party. Over the past few years, that rumor, completely baseless and easily resolved with a single web search, has grown louder and louder. If we speak up and deny it and correct it, the story gets bigger. If we don't respond to the false allegations at all, the story will still get bigger.

It's just part of the process that we, as an organization, will always be a target. For people in adjacent organizations and for people who want to cause us actual harm.

I have dedicated everything I have to this organization. Sometimes, more than I should have. People may see me on television or hear me on a podcast or on a TED Talk. You may think this is sweet. You don't see me grabbing my things and going to a safe house with my family because there are numerous credible threats on my life. You don't see me when a member of my family has been doxxed, again, and I have to make sure no harm comes to them.

Yes, I signed up for this. I am proud that I have. I knew what I was in for. Just because an organization becomes higher profile, it doesn't mean it becomes easier.

GUIDING QUESTIONS

1. Write down a time when you responded from a reactionary place.
2. What prompted the reaction and what was the outcome?
3. If you could take that same scenario and apply the response vs. reaction principle, how would the outcome be different?
4. How can you take this principle and practice it in your own abolitionist work?

Nothing Is Fixed

You have to act as if it were possible to radically transform the world. And you have to do it all the time.
—Angela Davis, February 13, 2014, SIU Carbondale
Van Nuys, Los Angeles, California 1993

I had always been a rule breaker, an experimenter, a challenger of normative structures. Even before I was sure about coming out as queer, I inherently knew my way of being wasn't wrong. Still, it was difficult to not feel shame for who I was. When I began working inside of movement spaces I craved a space that would see my differences as an asset rather than a liability.

When I became an organizer with the Bus Riders Union, an organization, much like New York's Straphangers Campaign, that represents public transportation users, I entered into a world where my way of being wasn't an isolated consequence of "bad" choices I had made. My first interaction with the organizers in training (OITs) at the Bus Riders Union was when I was being recruited by them. I was eighteen years old and two organizers came to speak to my youth leadership cohort. Both of them were young and dynamic. When they spoke, they spoke with a conviction that made me want to show up wherever they were. There was confidence, an electric sense of being that I felt lay dormant inside of me but was on its way to blooming.

They played the packed room a 20-minute short that highlighted the work of mainly women of color who were organizing and fighting back against the Los Angeles County transit system. The video showed badass women of color who were willing to take on a billion-dollar agency. Most importantly, all of the women were clearly charting a path away from social norms. I remember whispering to myself, "I want to be like them when I grow up."

Even the unofficial motto I heard sparked me. "One thousand more buses. One thousand less police." It was audacious and brave, and the moment I thought about how much that would change for people who depend on the transit system, it seemed like, well, of course this should happen.

Why should Black and Brown people, mostly low income, have to deal with overcrowded buses, difficult routes to employment and medical sites, poor schedules and high rates while white customers, smaller in number, had larger and more organized systems in their areas?

I joined the Bus Riders Union and spent over ten years in several different positions inside the organization. One thing I learned from the Bus Riders Union is that the only way to fight back in a city and county that is ruled by money is by experimenting and recognizing that nothing—and I mean nothing—is fixed.

When I say "fixed," I mean it in every sense of the word: nothing is permanent or absolute, and nothing within this current system has been repaired. The very first campaign I launched was a campaign ensuring that K–12 Los Angeles Unified School District students were able to easily access a student discount bus pass. When our campaign first challenged the Los Angeles Metro Board to disable the difficult process students needed to go through to get their bus passes, our campaign was met with silence. We waited weeks to hear from the elected official in charge of the Crenshaw District.

By week four, I knew they weren't going to contact us unless we did something major. With the help of one of the organizers at the Bus Riders Union, I contacted the principal at Crenshaw High School. The principal was willing to meet with me, and I asked the school if it would let me bring the bus pass campaign onto campus. I wanted to have my organization support students in getting their passes by walking them through the rigorous application process. The principal was grateful for our organization's efforts and let us on campus for the recess and lunch periods. I set up a digital camera and a printer to print the school photos, and I had a stack of pens and applications for students.

We signed up hundreds of students in one day and proved to the Metro Board that if a half-million-dollar organization like ours could support low-income students of color, their billion-dollar agency could certainly stop ignoring the requests of vulnerable students and do right by them.

We modeled this bus pass project in two more high schools. Whenever we signed up students, we would make sure the process was well documented, and then we would write a letter to the Metro Board and mail and fax them the number of students we signed up.

This was a campaign to both pressure the Metro Board to support students by implementing the protocol our bus pass campaign developed and to remind students of the power they have to change the course of history. Abolitionist experimentation opens up new possibilities.

Young people are particularly perceptive about making change. They think bigger than we do. We need to listen to them—and give them the tools they need. Ask a young burgeoning abolitionist you know: What needs to be changed? How do we change it?

The answers are phenomenal. Charlie and Hannah Lucas, from Georgia, developed an app called notOK to support people struggling with depression or other mental health issues. A person can click the digital panic button and a message will go out to a preselected group, along with that person's exact location, via GPS.

George Hofstetter, a teenager in California, developed the app CopStop, which is designed to help young people in their interactions with police and includes an option for filming police.

After years of hearing that they should be seen and not heard, young people all over the country and all over the world are proving that our ideas about what children can do are too narrow. Things that seem like they simply can't be done—are just waiting to be done.

These young people are transforming their worlds, which leads to an even wider appreciation for thinking outside of what you've been told to believe.

Think loud. What do you want to see changed? Now think of how some would say this system is fixed. Think of the reasons someone would tell you it can't be done. Then be ready to dismantle. Because all the things that are worth improving? Someone will tell you they're fixed.

To fix can mean to fasten. Just as something can be fastened, believe it can be unfastened, too.

The Montgomery Bus Boycott is another perfect example of people seeing that fixed behavior can be changed. Much like what was achieved with the Bus Riders Union, it's the kind of thing no one believes is possible until it happens.

People tend to forget some serious facts about the Montgomery Bus Boycott. First, let's not ever forget that Claudette Colvin, at 15 years old, was the person who actually set off the bus boycott. She was ready to be seen and heard after being arrested over not giving up her seat.

However, because she was young and pregnant, it was decided by the Civil Rights leaders of the time that someone the public would deem more respectable should represent the movement. Enter Rosa Parks, who re-created Colvin's situation. (Many versions of Parks's story leave out the fact that her protest was planned.) Claudette tells her own story in the book *Claudette Colvin: Twice Toward Justice*.

It's understandable that the Civil Rights leaders did what they believed to be necessary at the time. Another interesting factoid: when the boycott was first announced, the Black people of Montgomery did not even ask for segregation to end on the buses. They wanted the hiring of Black drivers and simple courtesy—a first-come, first-seated policy, with the understanding that Black people would *still enter through the rear.*

Even though boycott leaders were trying to make change, their thinking was still fixed in many ways at the very beginning. Perhaps they believed that asking for everything they deserved would be too much. Perhaps they believed the discrimination was too fixed in some ways. Perhaps it was.

The Montgomery Bus Boycott lasted 381 days, more than a full year. The strength of the people is still something to behold. Folks were walking and carpooling for months and months. I can't even imagine how often the people involved thought that things were fixed and that this boycott might not work. Black cabdrivers lowered their fares to match bus fare so that people could get to work, and they picked up as many boycotters as they could. They made it work.

Compare yourself to abolitionists before you. Looking back, did they consider how to protest as fixed? Did they consider what they could achieve as fixed? Is there any place in your life as an abolitionist that you realize you are still thinking of as fixed?

What to Read/Watch/See/Hear: *Creative Quest* by Ahmir "Questlove" Thompson, of The Roots. This book, about the power of creativity and how we can put it into practice, illustrates a lighthearted and yet firmly powerful way to approach goals. Creativity and expansion of the mind are intrinsically linked, and this is a book that shows—through one person's lens—how they can elevate us.

What I Know: I have to remind myself that I have a privilege of having done this work for a really long time. I'm 37, but I've seen and done a lot of this work, and some of it—and how it must be done—comes easily to me. However, I know that I have to break this down to those who are either just coming to this work or perhaps returning. I have to explain that working with the Bus Riders Union while still watching my mom deal with being disfellowshipped from the Jehovah's Witnesses gave me a unique perspective on what is fixed. Also, geographically, coming up in a place like California, much like New York or anywhere up and down the east and west coasts, gave me access to thinkers and do-ers I may not have met or worked with if I lived in less populated or more conservative rural places.

I also know that money matters when we talk about things being fixed. I grew up poor. Poor enough to feel it. (Sometimes, young poor people live in households that get by just well enough that they don't feel it. That was not my life.)

Being poor feels *very* fixed. So, it's hard to see anything changing when you are looking through that prism. When you're a poor Jehovah's Witness, you take some of the little money you make and give it to the Kingdom without really understanding why. If you attend a church where it's expected that you follow prosperity theology, you may give because everything is fixed and you feel it's the only way to do better. Even if you make a decent living, feeding children and getting back and forth to a job is at the forefront of your mind, so you just do what you're told.

What You Know: In order to see things around you as not fixed, you will have to see things within you as not fixed. Example: A 2020 study from Queen's University in Canada calculated a typical person has about 6,000 thoughts every day, and for most of us, 80 percent of those thoughts are negative. If this is even partly true, if even just 50 percent of our thoughts are negative, how can we manage to change the idea that certain things are fixed? We have to figure out how to think more positively in order to see these things as unfixed. Negative thoughts are often one-dimensional narratives that have no potential to evolve or develop. Thinking positively means reorienting these one-dimensional stories toward a framework that allows for more possibility, where these stories can transform into different narratives. It's easier said than done, of course, but knowing what we need to do makes it easier. I want to make the distinction here that this practice is not toxic positivity. We cannot positively think racism away, for example, but positive thoughts allow us to orient ourselves around what is possible.

Those Who Can Show: Ruth Gilmore is an abolitionist icon who has been instrumental in collecting, archiving and legitimizing the tenets of the anti-carceral movement. Ruth was born in 1950 in New Haven, Connecticut, into a family that was keen on the importance of being involved in social justice efforts that tackled dismantling all inequalities. Her father was a union organizer and local leader in her town, and so Ruthie, from a very early age, was exposed to the power of community organizing and how these movements could shift policy. As she got older, Gilmore worked as a mechanic, then an actor, and eventually paved her way into the world of academia. She was among the first women to gain admission to Yale University, where she studied dramatic literature and criticism and earned her B.A. and M.A. At the age of 43, she pursued her Ph.D. at Rutgers, the State University of New Jersey, where she dove into the discipline of geography. Gilmore was particularly interested in studying with Neil Smith, a renowned scholar on geography, social theory and urban anthropology. As the trajectory of her career shows, Gilmore has had a variety of interests, all of which have led her back to the heart of her work, which is to challenge this idea that prisons are "the all-purpose use of cages to solve social, political and economic problems."

For Gilmore, nothing has ever been fixed.

Gilmore identifies as a prison activist and prison scholar—her distinct role is to intervene and complicate the conversations happening within academia in order to further transform the larger public conversation about abolition. Gilmore essentially created the study of carceral geography, which examines the "interrelationships between landscapes, natural resources, political economy, infrastructure and the policing, jailing, caging and controlling of populations." When Gilmore began this investigative work, this field of study was dominated by the white supremacist, capitalist and patriarchal values that had begun the study of geography so many years before her.

The same values that glorify colonization as "civilization" were used to justify the systemic removal and erasure of indigenous people from their land and the pillaging of the earth in the name of "progress." Gilmore challenged these antiquated values and experimented with the entire approach to geography by questioning the uses and methodology of academic findings.

Through her work, Gilmore began a conversation with thinkers such as Cedric Robinson, who was pioneering the study and analysis of the Black radical tradition, and Barbara Smith, who was building and popularizing Black Feminism in the United States. Gilmore was particularly interested in examining the prison industrial complex and sought to use the field of carceral geography to build a case for dismantling the prison system. Gilmore has been at the front lines of prison abolition for 30 years, and her book *Golden Gulag: Prisons, Surplus, Crisis, and Opposition in Globalizing California* is an abolitionist classic text that has been referenced time and again to challenge the effectiveness of the carceral system with hard data and analysis from experts like her. In her book, Gilmore analyzes the economic changes and policies that led to the expansion of California prisons in the twentieth century. In addition, Gilmore explores the ways in which community organizing has effectively raised awareness of the prison system and, consequently, built the infrastructure to enable the most vulnerable and marginalized people to fight against it.

According to The Sentencing Project, there has been a 1 percent annual decline in the US prison population since 2009. In California, from 2005 to 2015, there was a 29 percent decrease in the prison population.

Clearly, the groundbreaking work of Gilmore continues to make an impact in this fight for liberation. In 1997 Gilmore and her longtime comrade, Angela Davis, co-founded Critical Resistance—an organization that is building a movement "challenging the idea that imprisonment and policing are a solution for social, political, and economic problems." Critical Resistance has been the hub for many abolitionists over the years, and it is this think tank that is the political home of many abolitionists today. Gilmore's life is an exceptional example of how to be fearless and creative when we challenge these seemingly fixed systems we are born into. She teaches us that changing the world is part of the legacy of resistance and resilience we are invited to step into as the stewards of the next generation.

How We'll Grow: So much of the campaign work I did in my youth and as an adult required us to experiment. We are often trapped in ideologies of what an individual can do and what their communities are allowed to do. Our BIPOC, disabled and poor communities are relegated into silence. We aren't given a platform to fight for our needs. Hell, we are told we don't have needs and must just accept what is given to us. When we experiment individually and collectively, our possibilities open up. My queerness opened up my possibilities on how and who I love, and it also informed how I fight and who I fight for. Experimenting has been a survival tool for so many communities. The more we can let go of our obsession with rigidity and the rules some white wealthy men made up, the more we can ground ourselves in a future of plurality.

When we choose experimentation as abolitionists, we get to see what's possible on the other side of the rules that have been written for us. Abolitionists who have experimented throughout the development of this nation have changed the course of history. If we didn't experiment, the project of chattel slavery would still exist. Jim Crow and Black codes would still exist. It is because of our experimentation that the abolitionist movement in its current form continues to disrupt the police and prison state.

The Real World: The media can sometimes feel like the one thing that is absolutely fixed. As much as our organization (and our personal lives) can be affected by the media, we need it. We need publicity surrounding our events. We need social media to meet people where they are. We need the media—all forms of it. Yet, we must all critique and keep certain publications at a distance. Media matters.

When the mainstream media comes calling, how do you navigate? If the founders of BLM are on the cover of *TIME* magazine, what does that mean? Are we spreading our message? Are we publicizing our personal brands? Are we giving legitimacy to a corporation that doesn't deserve it? Some days, I can answer *yes* to all of those questions. Some days I can answer *no*. The truth is, you'll have to work with your organization when it comes to the media because sometimes it just has to be done. Yet, I have turned down documentaries on major networks to maintain my personal schedule, including parenting, yoga and therapy, and if the time and circumstances had not been right, we would have turned down *TIME*, too. We huddle and think: does this help us? If this in any way supports a system that we work against, how do we make sense of it and move forward (or not)? It's a constant juggle to make sure we get it right, and we don't always get it right. Because, yup, nothing is fixed.

GUIDING QUESTIONS

1. How has experimenting worked for you in the work that you do?
2. Name a time you had to lean into experimentation? What was the outcome?
3. How have you bought into social norms and how have they inhibited your ability to be present for your work?
4. Name three things you can do today to help you experiment with your movement work.

Say Yes to Imagination

Science fiction is simply a way to practice the future together. I suspect that is what many of you are up to, practicing futures together, practicing justice together, living into new stories. It is our right and responsibility to create a new world.

—adrienne maree brown, *Emergent Strategy: Shaping Change, Changing Worlds*

As a child, I usually walked home from school. Today, many children no longer walk back and forth to school, or anywhere else in their communities. For safety reasons and otherwise. On one hand, walking was good for me, physically, and as a way to wind down from the day at school and have my own private thoughts.

The thing about walking from school in a neighborhood like mine was that I literally felt like I was under siege. Police were the omnipresent feature. As I made my way home and I crossed into my mostly Black and Brown working-class neighborhood, my body would tense up and my stomach would be in knots. The police were incredibly unpredictable and their presence never made me feel secure or safe.

Each block they roamed felt tense, like our community was being hunted.

Sometimes I would wonder, had I done something wrong? Were they on their way to my house? Would I see more officers once I got closer to home? Once I got to my house, I would finish up my schoolwork, and my mom would let us watch 30 minutes of television a day before we would head off to bed. I was a child. Even though we didn't have much in the way of material things, I should have had room to breathe and fall asleep and dream. I should not have felt a tightening in my chest because my neighborhood was always surrounded. The flash of blue and red lights streaming into my bedroom all night should not have been my nightlight. With the sounds of sirens all around me, instead of falling asleep, I would spend hours gazing at my ceiling, imagining the kind of place where I wished my family and community could live.

I didn't imagine luxury. I didn't imagine butlers and swimming pools and fancy clothes. I didn't imagine white gloves and tea-length dresses. I didn't imagine servants and my mother doing nothing and still having money.

I couldn't imagine that broadly. I simply imagined the things that would allow my mother to be fully joyful. She spent much of her motherhood working three jobs and fighting off the state from swallowing her children alive. I know that she was exhausted by the consistent police harassment and attacks on my siblings—my brother Monte, in particular.

I would imagine a world where our family received food on a regular basis, access to green space and after-school activities and programming, where my mom could spend time with us instead of having to commit herself to 18-hour workdays. I wanted my family and community to live in a neighborhood not riddled by police, and I wanted to be able to get help and support and resources for my and my community's dreams. I wanted my community to have access to beauty and food and adequate public education. I wanted to know that we were not going to just survive but that my community would thrive.

Wanting the very bare minimum to exist on this planet should not even be called *imagining*. It is the work of abolition to make sure that young BIPOC are not using their imagination to wish for clean water and books for school.

Abolitionist praxis offers us an opportunity to dream of a world where our families and communities are provided with the utmost care. Abolitionist praxis exists in a world where our governments are no longer reliant on police, jails, prisons, courts and military. Abolitionist praxis is rooted in our collective healing. It is rooted in a deep and profound trust for all beings and our ability to love each other. While we sit in this moment during this global pandemic, we get to reimagine an abolitionist world. We owe it to each other and ourselves. We owe it to our descendants and it all starts with our imagination.

I once read that people will always lean toward joyful things. So we must make seeking justice joyful. Where is that world? We live in it. We just have to imagine it.

The world we currently live in is based on an economy of punishment rather than an economy of care. Its economy is rooted in 400 years of harm and violence toward a community that was stolen from its homeland and brought to build this country. This economy of punishment perpetuates the killing, harming, maiming, abuse, violation and sexual abuse of Black people with little to no accountability. We have spent 400 years in the white supremacist patriarchal imagination. Four hundred years of torture. Four hundred years of abuse. Four hundred years of sadism. Four hundred years of despair. Four hundred years of greed. Four hundred years of devastation. When we center the abolitionist imagination we are actively opposing the current economy of punishment and dreaming up an economy of care that is grounded in love and compassion for true imagining of public safety—not a public safety that is predicated on the unsafety of Black people.

bell hooks broke down what this racist economy looks like in our society today. She said in a speech: "I began to use the phrase in my work 'white supremacist capitalist patriarchy' because I wanted to have some language that would actually remind us continually of the interlocking systems of domination that define our reality."

The important word here from hooks is *continually*. The white supremacist capitalist patriarchy is the lens through which we filter all of our experiences. It has been for all of our lives.

It's pervasive. None of us, except perhaps those who live completely off the grid, are capable of escaping white supremacist capitalist patriarchy. Are you living in the world and doing abolitionist work? Are you aware of how your day-to-day choices support white supremacist capitalist patriarchy? Start your day by making your own free-trade pour-over in a handmade coffee pot? It's still connected to white supremacy, from the sugar that comes from sugar cane plantations to the Amazon corporation that delivers your handmade coffeepot. Every moment of our day is a constant balance of living and understanding why and how we're living. Where are your clothes from? What are you driving? What are you eating? What shows are you watching? Who made your phone? Who controls the internet you can access on that phone? What's really happening to the things you recycle and where do they end up?

Yes, it can be overwhelming. Much of abolition work is. It's up to you to figure out what you sacrifice and what you don't. No one is making a daily tally of your commitment. (Actually, some people might be. I know some are committed to tallying what I do. Gotta let that go.)

All we can do is be ever vigilant and aware. Whether it's watching football or eating pizza, there's a level of white supremacist capitalist patriarchy that we are supporting. If you're aware, you can make tiny—and then major—changes. Then help others do the same.

I asked a friend to check in with her 13-year-old on something she knows she has to sacrifice in the name of not supporting white supremacist patriarchy. The teen responded that she really wanted a certain pair of Mary Janes. She found them on a site that she knew was owned by racists who had horrible attitudes toward the LGBTQIA+ community, so the teen made the decision not to buy the shoes.

(My friend helped her out by sourcing the shoes at a nearby thrift shop. Win-win!)

This same friend has a partner who watches the NFL. He knows full well that it's supporting everything that's wrong with white supremacy. The NFL is an organization that has not supported Colin Kaepernick, has a dearth of Black coaches, and has been consistently racist since its founding in 1920.

Dr. Robert Turner is an assistant professor in the department of clinical research and leadership at the George Washington University School of Medicine and Health Sciences. His book *Not for Long* explains racism in the NFL and how it affects current and former players. According to his research, Black men, who make up just 6 percent of the population, comprise 70 percent of NFL players. The average player makes about two million dollars per year, ten times less than owners. Then they leave the sport in grave risk of developing chronic traumatic encephalopathy (CTE). The lives and bodies of Black men are risked every season, and the NFL owners and management could not care less.

They don't care about representation, either. In 2002, the NFL enacted the Rooney Rule. Football teams have to interview at least two "ethnic minorities" for vacancies in senior-level positions. Just interview them, not actually hire. That was almost 20 years ago. How many Black and Latinx head coaches are in the NFL this season? *Three.* Yet, her partner watches, knowing how disrespectful the NFL is toward its players.

How do we exist within this framework? How do we make sense of it and slice into it and keep abolitionist ideals? We can't judge Black men who watch the NFL. We all have our own things with similarly problematic ideals.

For me, for many of us, we try the best we can to make the moves we need to make—especially when it comes to the media. I have a development deal with Warner Bros. Entertainment Inc. to make sure people who look like me and my people are represented in the media. Like hooks said in her conversation, there is so much in pop culture that is damaging to our communities but that has become part of our methodology. We see women dismiss and attack each other in the name of supposed reality. We are blocking and canceling people, even our friends, instead of mending fences and having healing, courageous conversations. Whoever is the loudest, meanest, most ruthless and most comical in the room will rule.

I want the projects created in my Warner Bros. deal to counter all of that. Here's what else I understand. The original Warner Bros. studio, founded by four brothers, Harry, Albert, Sam and Jack Warner, didn't do much to ensure that our people were properly represented. There's a collection of animations, called the "Censored Eleven," that are deeply rooted in racist imagery—and it's completely owned by the company my new production outfit is connected to.

This is a fact. It's still my job to make this relationship work for my people, my ideals and my mission statement. I would never say that every decision we make to confront racist patriarchy behavior will be the right one—or will not be fraught with other contradictions. All I can say—and encourage you to do—is to *continually* center your purpose when you're doing abolitionist decision making. There's always more we can do, for sure. The ideal is to just try our best and stay aware.

Imagining beyond the status quo is one of the cornerstones of the principles of abolition.

For many years, the idea of abolishing prisons and defunding the police was dismissed as laughable. Even some in the community who worked on the front lines believed this to be *too* dramatic. *Let's not be ridiculous here.* We don't have a choice but to have police. Who will help our children in school, the good cops, the safety patrol officers? It took someone else to dream bigger and imagine. Why not a school where we don't need armed soldiers who are not invested in the community? How about a school where families and staff are supported and have what they need?

In a city in New Jersey, a friend shared with me that she saw something completely disheartening as a substitute teacher. A student in second grade, a very typical second grader, began acting out. He disrupted the lesson more than once. He yelled out of turn. None of the teacher's warnings changed his behavior.

An administrator saw the commotion in the classroom and came inside. My friend said all of those seven-year-olds froze, abject terror on their faces. The administrator said someone would be coming to deal with the student who was out of line.

It ended up being the school's "safety resource officer." An armed, uniformed police officer.

He came into that classroom and told the seven-year-old to come with him. The class was terrified, the child was terrified. The officer looked bored, like he removed seven-year-olds from their classrooms every day.

Because he did.

Thirty-eight of the 39 schools in that particular city have armed, uniformed officers. Statistics show that schools that have these officers are far more likely to have students arrested, and children of color are more likely to be arrested.

The substitute teacher found out later that this young student had been told that morning that his mother would be losing custody of him and a DYFS counselor would be picking him up that afternoon to place him with a foster family. He was going to be separated from his four siblings who were also students in the same school. He wanted to see his brothers before he left for the day to go to another family.

This is an extreme case, but there is no reason why the staff should not have been able to be present for this child. A police officer is not equipped to deal with his emotions.

Sometimes, a kid who is misbehaving needs a hug. Sometimes, they need a meal. Sometimes, they need a conversation. They never, ever need interaction with police officers.

Why can't we imagine a world where seven-year-olds don't have to interact with armed guards if they're having a bad day?

If this country spends *trillions* on prisons, why can't we imagine a world where we don't need them—and have a better system in place?

What happens if people receive free, quality health care as a basic human right? What happens if a community can design and receive the budget needed for its school system? What if we don't have to align with a fixed approach to marriage in order to share benefits? What if instead of the police, we had a council of elders, respected from within the community, who could intervene with binding policies?

It's only taken 400 years to get here. We can imagine a world where humans are treated with dignity, care and respect.

David Walker, an eighteenth-century abolitionist, took to his printing press to share his abolitionist ideals with the world.

His publication, *Walker's Appeal,* used imagination.

He invoked the ire of abolitionists, both Black and white, who didn't want to go as far as he knew abolition needed to go. He was radical. He had thoughts and ideas and plans that went far beyond what others thought was possible. Let's use Walker as an example of how we must persist. Even when people don't believe in your vision, if it's a vision that's about forwarding healing, justice and dignity, then it's a vision worth fighting for.

What to Read/Watch/See/Hear: *The Radical Imagination: Social Movement Research in the Age of Austerity* by Alex Khasnabish and Max Haiven. The idea of imagination being radical is explored here as well as what it means for movement work if we continually turn our imagination up to radical levels. Radical imagination has worked in the past (Wait! Maybe the Earth is *not* flat!), and all of our other disciplines—science, math and beyond—dovetail with the idea of imagining radically.

What I Know: In 1971, in a televised interview, writers and activists James Baldwin and Nikki Giovanni met and spoke for hours on every subject under the sun. It is a remarkable showcase of generational ideals and imagination, and every minute of is still completely relevant today. I urge you to search for it on YouTube and watch it completely.

Baldwin and Giovanni have always been more than writers, their hot knife of words continually slicing through the butter of ideas like racism, white supremacy and social justice. They are warriors, not just artists.

They imagined a different world while also working toward putting that world in place.

At ten years old, Baldwin suffered abuse at the hands of the New York Police Department. This was in 1934. These interactions with law enforcement would continue through his teens. Baldwin noted these things. He wrote about these things. He defined these things. He spoke about these things. Often, imagining a world without negativity begins by acknowledging the negativity that abounds. Baldwin did this—always.

"I knew I was black, of course, but I also knew I was smart," said Baldwin to Giovanni. "I didn't know how I would use my mind, or even if I could, but that was the only thing I had to use."

At a very young age, Baldwin had to expand his mind, use his imagination. That ability would guide him throughout his life and career.

When Baldwin was still a young man in Harlem, a white teacher noticed his talents as a playwright and offered to take him to see a play on Broadway. His stepfather was outraged and his mother was reluctant to let him go. Again, this was the 1930s. A white teacher voluntarily coming to their Harlem apartment, to take their son on an outing?

This is where imagination comes in. Baldwin's stepfather did not want him to go. The only thing he could imagine was harm coming to young James or judgment from others in his community. If anyone should be able to expose young James to the arts, if anyone should have the money or the time, it should be his parents. James's mother had a different way of imagining. She was uncomfortable, as well, but she also knew her son was talented and that she and her husband might not be able to get him as far as he needed to go. Baldwin's mother vetoed her husband and let Baldwin go to the play with his white teacher. It was the first of many serendipitous acts of imagining—his or someone else's—that would shape his career. His careful cataloguing of these moments has helped us in the present day to continue to imagine, as well.

Like many of us (myself and my family especially included), Baldwin's life of imagining was at first limited to religious experiences. This is not to say that religion doesn't play its part in developing our minds for social justice (for better or for worse). However, in its most stringent forms, it can definitely limit us. For Baldwin, after early years of growing closer to a role in the ministry, he felt it was stunting his ability to think deeper and further. He spent the rest of his creative and personal life non-religious.

While a teenager, he had dabbled in the arts, including editing his school paper. A friend told him about an artist whose studio was near Baldwin's after-school job. The artist was Beauford Delaney, a Black man, originally from Knoxville, Tennessee, who was a modernist painter fully entrenched in the Harlem Renaissance.

Delaney became a mentor to Baldwin. At the time, Baldwin was already an artist. He was firmly on his path, and yet, he couldn't quite see it. He didn't yet *imagine* it. Until he began to watch Delaney, not just in his craft but in his world. He saw how Delaney carried himself, the people he surrounded himself with, the people he mentored, like Baldwin himself. Delaney stretched himself. He used his talents to stretch others. After working with him, Baldwin wrote that he could see it—he could see what being an artist actually looked like. He could imagine it.

As you continue the promise of learning to imagine, remember that someone else could very well be watching you to learn the same thing.

Another space where James Baldwin and many other creative activists share the same push to imagine is the idea of becoming an expat. Baldwin, Josephine Baker, Delaney and many others boarded planes to Paris with not much money or firm plans, knowing the city would welcome them. They were able to imagine the idea of having a space to be free—and yet to continue to plan for revolution in their homeland. (We'll discuss later how revolution can be put forth no matter where you are, on the front lines or in a cubicle 3,000 miles away from the protest.)

To imagine is not always to imagine progress and achievement. It is often to imagine how things can go off the rails, can go against everything you know and believe. Baldwin, for example, found himself writing a piece he could have never imagined. In his 1972 book *No Name in the Street,* he writes about the life and death of three close friends whom he'd also known professionally. Martin Luther King Jr., Medgar Evers and Malcolm X were all killed in the late sixties, each death hitting Baldwin deeper than the last. In the heat of the movement, you know that stakes are high. All three of those men prophesied their own deaths. King did so literally one night before his assassination. Baldwin had to feel it in the air. Could he have imagined that these people would die so soon, beginning in 1963 and ending in 1968? Could he have even imagined where things would go in just five years?

While he mourned, he was an activist. He wrote enough about race and social justice that the FBI began to keep a file on him and his work. His writing had him watched much more closely than other Black writers. Richard Wright, author of *Native Son*, had 276 pages in his file. Baldwin had almost two thousand.

When Baldwin passed away from stomach cancer, Toni Morrison eulogized him in *The New York Times*. She said Baldwin's death was not a calamity. Quite the opposite, she said it was a time for jubilee. She believed in a final act of imagining that Baldwin had left for us all. Morrison believed that Baldwin had left us all with a crown we could imagine wearing at all times, as we moved forward in our journeys.

"'Our crown,' you said, 'has already been bought and paid for. All we have to do,' you said, 'is wear it.'"

Baldwin's idea of wearing crowns bought and paid for by previous generations is one of the best ways to define and illustrate the idea of imagining. Put your crown on and think big.

What You Know: Recently I had a conversation with someone who shared a sharp example of how and what it means to imagine. To think bigger and beyond. Alexandra graduated from an HBCU and pledged the sorority that many in her family had belonged to. After many years of formal education, she went into a series of jobs with higher and higher profiles in both economics and law. After a marriage, a divorce and two children, she continued to climb the ladder, though she was more and more disillusioned and bored. She also believed she would do more in social justice reform, but her hands were tied at her job and she was exhausted in her personal life.

What Alexandra had always wanted to do was be a hairstylist with her own salon. From age five, she'd felt it was her thing. It's what she imagined. Unfortunately, when she shared, she was told she was not imagining big enough.

This is the tricky thing about imagination. It's *yours* to interpret. No one else can tell you it's too big—or not big enough. Because of cultural norms, it would have been near impossible to convince her parents to allow her to graduate with near-perfect SAT scores and several full college scholarships on the table—and go to cosmetology school. In her forties, her imagination began to hum again.

She left her job after saving enough to support

herself and her children for a full year. During that time, she went to cosmetology school and then began working on her 1,600 hours to get her license.

This story could end with Alexandra working as a hairstylist. That would be fine if it were so. But the story is a bit more expanded than that. She opened a salon in her community, and she hired other stylists and barbers from the community. On nights and weekends, her salon was a hub for creative people, including writers and poets. Sunday mornings, there were tutorials offered for high school students. After some time, Alexandra was able to put into place one of her biggest dreams—offering free styling for men and women in transition: those leaving relationships, released from prison or recovering from health issues. Within five years, she was in a space that she'd fully imagined. She didn't make $350,000, as she had before. What she did make was a life, a life she'd imagined.

Yes, you need to think big. But be careful about what you think *big* should look like. Only you can determine what your imagination should bring to you. If Alexandra were a hairstylist who dreamed of practicing law, then going to law school and making her way up that ladder would be her mission and her plan and her imagination.

Whatever and however you believe you will do best by your imagination, that's your path. In addition to being flexible with your own life, make sure you try to have that flexibility for others in your life. If you have a should-be college student who is actually a would-be salon owner, keep that flexibility in your imagination.

Those Who Can Show: adrienne maree brown, author, facilitator, sci-fi enthusiast and pleasure activist, has written and spoken about the imagination and the work of imagining new systems extensively. Her belief is that we can and must imagine a new world, because for the people at the margins—Black, Queer, disabled men and women and trans men and women, the poor and people of color—our lives depend on our ability to connect to our pleasure, what brings us joy and inspires us to dream bigger. brown identifies as an Afrofuturist, and much of her philosophy is influenced by the impetus and the proclamations that Black life exists in the future—and it exists extravagantly, limitlessly and freely.

brown was born in El Paso, Texas, to an interracial couple who fell in love in the 1970s in the deep South, where interracial dating was still believed to be socially repugnant. Interracial marriage had only very recently been made legal in the United States. Still, their love made the seemingly impossible possible—and in just three months of courtship, Jane and Jerry married. For brown, this intimate love story has been the "guideline of her life": to channel love to make the impossible possible. Her father was in the military, and so she and her family spent much of her early years traveling the world—experiencing varied degrees of racism everywhere they went.

Her experiences in the military environment were

her first lessons in holding contradictions as she became increasingly aware of her positionality as a Black, queer woman. brown moved out of her home and enrolled at Columbia University, where she studied African American studies, political science and voice. brown was an undergrad when Amadou Diallo was killed by police officers, and she credits this as the critical moment when her politicization and deep commitment to transforming the world was solidified. brown continued to harness her skills as she worked as a harm reduction specialist, working with substance users and sex workers. She then moved to doing electoral work—"harm reduction on a national scale," as she refers to it. She speaks fondly of her work with the Ruckus Society, where she felt she could show up as her whole self, and the "liberating experience" of working as a facilitator of social justice meetings.

In her time as a facilitator with the Ruckus Society, she noticed a pattern in her conversations with these powerful organizers, policy makers, and people who were invested in changing the world: there was a "deep crisis of imagination and vision." She noticed that oftentimes people could readily diagnose, analyze and tell a whole history about the problems in our society—but rarely could they envision the world beyond the pain of injustice. Even more alarming, she observed that the well-meaning people in the room were quick to separate themselves from the "bad people" and place all blame on the "other" without taking our human interconnectedness into consideration.

In her time at the Ruckus Society, a few important things were solidified for brown: as freedom fighters we must lean into our interdependence, we must be able to reconstruct as well as we are able to deconstruct, and we must always, as she reminds us, be "cultivating the muscle of radical imagination needed to dream beyond fear."

This framework has catapulted her into building on her new body of work as a pleasure activist.

It is her belief that "human beings always choose the path of pleasure," and in order to entice humans to fight for and create more experiences of justice, we have to "make justice the most pleasurable experience a human can involve themselves in." This charge that brown is declaring is the practice of vision and imagination that centers humans showing up as their full selves in order to ideate collaboratively and create comprehensive solutions to our most grave societal problems.

This pivot is critical in our work because, historically, we have been conditioned to believe that there is a mythical utopian endpoint in this movement for justice where everyone is happy and holding hands. The trouble with that is that change is constant, there are differing points of view, and distinct needs for everyone—so this one utopian vision could never satisfy everyone. brown urges us to "practice variance" and to experience our beauty and humanity at every single condition we find ourselves in as we experiment with what works.

As we articulate this compelling and irresistible vision, brown reminds us to have more curiosity and more grace as we practice, at the most personal level, what we want to see at the systemic level. This is where the most powerful transformation begins—how we move toward right relationships with our families, friends and community. brown's presence of vision and her ability to inspire us to find joy and pleasure as we challenge this dystopian system have cultivated a deep yearning in so many of us to lead with imagination as a critical part of our strategy. Her book *Emergent Strategy* serves to chart our current movement, where transforming our world is not only possible but a "science of emergence: relational, adaptive, interdependent, decentralized, and transformative at every level of our relationships." Divergence, emergence and pleasure are not only welcomed but critical as we rewrite the trajectory of our human relationship to this ecosystem. brown continues to model and cultivate this yearning as part of our collective political and strategic framework.

We practice building our imagination because so much of the work of building a new future that is not rooted in punishment depends on it. Our imagination provides a new pathway toward building out what is possible. We assume that everything we see in front of us right now has always existed. But it hasn't. Imagining is not just closing your eyes to escape what is presently happening. The kind of imagining I am calling for is active, involved and creative. We have to reroute what we are and what we see. I am calling for you to start imagining what your creed will be. It is also about what we see in the future. Imagining is actually at the center of this work. We are often unable to see what is possible, and we are wedded to a particular way of being. Fear drives our actions. Cop and jail propaganda have inundated what we believe is true about law enforcement and incarceration. Every single cop show has captured the imagination of people across the world. We have been taught to believe that cops are the good guys and jails keep us safer. We have been implicated in white people's fearful imagination of us.

So we proactively practice a new world that centers human, plant and being dignity. A world where children can play free of violence and turbulence. We practice grace and commitment to each other. We prioritize people over profit. We practice so one day a generation of babies will grow up to be adults who no longer bear the burden of having to make a system and the people in that system see them. We practice so we can feel the true aliveness of being joyful and living inside of our strength. Not the strength that forces you to be an adult far too early, but the strength of our legacy. We practice imagination so we can be fulfilled inside of the collective.

Sometimes, we think of imagination as child's play. Children are supposed to dream and imagine and adults are supposed to think forward and be level-headed. But the best kind of forward thinking is steeped in imagination. We have to remind ourselves that it's never time to stop imagining.

How We'll Grow: How do we practice this? Just like with respond vs. react, keeping a pen and notebook nearby will help. Try to catch a negative thought as it happens. You're late to work. A plan for radical change seems like it's being thwarted. A case of injustice doesn't seem to have an easy solution—or any solution at all. Before your brain gets to *this will never work,* try writing down the conflict. What's going on? How is it making you feel? What is the best-case scenario? Without thinking about what could go wrong, think about what could go right. Write down how you imagine it could go.

Get granular with this practice. Are you getting your hair or nails done? What does your imagination tell you about the right color or style? Not your brain. Your imagination. What does a beauty choice have to do with social justice and dismantling white supremacy? If it helps you broaden your imagination and the choices you make, it has everything to do with it.

Let's say you're thinking about your next job. You know that you need to make significantly more money, but you haven't calculated what that actually looks like or how to make it happen. You look up the average salary for the position. You ask your mentor and others in the field. You research and you crunch the numbers. What happens if you just ask for what you want? Not what you're qualified to receive. Not what a website or a mentor says it's fair to ask for. What would make you happy? What would make you leave the interview smiling ear to ear? Whatever *that* number is, imagine asking for it.

I am not going to tell you that you'll get double what you're asking for at your next interview (though it *has* happened). What I am telling you to do is start to take thoughts as they come, stop, stretch your imagination, and see where it goes.

I'll give an example from a friend. She was having trouble staying off social media while she completed an important project. She began researching apps that would block the sites that distract her. She was tough on herself for not being able to stay off the sites on her own. Instead of going down a road of negativity, she decided to imagine what a world untethered from social media would look like. She wasn't interested in logging off the sites permanently. They were helpful and useful in moderation. She decided to imagine what her digital world would look like if she could dream hard enough. At first, she thought of handwriting her work so she would have no reason to get online. While that was lofty, it wasn't realistic. Then she thought, what if she just didn't have any apps or even internet access installed on her computer at all? What if she took her computer down to factory settings and didn't install social media or even search engines? Was it even possible? Since she worked on a word processing system that autosaved to cloud-based storage, how would she do her work?

It turns out that even as she began to work out in her mind how unplugging *could* work, she began to spend less time on the distracting sites. Eventually, she did take her computer down to factory settings, but she remained online so she could back up her work. Just imagining a world that was easier to navigate—made it easier to navigate.

On top of that, she spread the word. She reconfigured her friend's laptop. At first her friend was not pleased, but she immediately noticed that her creative work was being prioritized. That she was less stressed in general. The concept of imagination caught hold of her friend, who took it a step further. She now powers her phone down during the workday, even though she's at home. They shared this practice with their friend group. Both of them said that their entire household has fewer dings and rings, fewer notifications, fewer people diving for their phones in the middle of dinner. It all spread out from one person thinking beyond apps to keep them from being distracted. (I mean, these apps likely work. But downloading an app to keep you from going on apps? There's a moment that's ripe for non-reformist reform. We'll get back to that.)

Formal education is another place where imagination is also being stretched. (Another place for non-reformist reform. Again, we'll return here.)

For hundreds of years, we've placed our students in school from kindergarten through twelfth grade. The curriculum has had very little imagination, and where you are socioeconomically dictates the quality of the education you receive.

I was one of the lucky ones. In many ways my education was experimental and shaped me into becoming an abolitionist. We're not all fortunate enough to attend these schools or have our children in these schools. There have been others who have needed to do this sort of work on their own, using imagination to set the curriculum.

There is a theory called *unschooling* or *deschooling* that operates within a unique paradigm shift: people can lead and develop their own curriculum using their own curiosity and imagination.

Imagine asking a school-aged child on a Monday morning, "What do you want to learn about today?" What would happen if you told them they would not be going to school that day and instead would learn about anything they wanted to?

Over and over again, students have answered this question with insight, imagination and ideas that extend far beyond what their state-sanctioned curriculums would expect and require.

"How come the sun can't be blue and the skies be yellow?"

"How can I make my own game like *Fortnite*?"

"Why does it take so long to make a vaccine for Covid-19?"

"What happens if the president doesn't leave before Biden goes to the White House?"

"How do you make chocolate?"

A fellow writer got all of these questions from her 13-year-old at the beginning of quarantine, while her school was closed and they were waiting for virtual instruction to begin. All she did was tell her daughter, "Go for it, learn it all." She moved out of the way and just made sure her child had all the things she'd need to get the answers. There were a few trips to places like a beauty supply store, a home improvement store. But for the most part, this kid developed and executed her own curriculum. There was some shaping done by the parent, but it was very light.

For art, the child decided to paint a portrait of Frida Kahlo, her favorite artist, onto a pair of pants. Her favorite artists on Instagram often paint onto clothing, and she decided she'd give it a try. With all the prep work and sketching that goes into such a project, she never found time to try it out under her traditional school schedule, which included pages and pages of busywork to be done after school. The things she learned, the way her imagination had to be stretched in order to get that painting done, still lined up with her traditional curriculum.

- ENGLISH: The young woman started out by reading about Frida Kahlo and her influences. There were a few memoirs that she read excerpts from, and on her own time, she was able to finish them while taking notes on what would be necessary for her project. She was not just reading for a test that would expect her to regurgitate factoids.

- SOCIAL STUDIES: The student watched a documentary on Kahlo's life and further explored how she would pay tribute to Kahlo's work.
- SCIENCE: The student needed to determine the correct density of acrylic paint when using denim as a canvas. She had to carefully approach the project like a scientific experiment, following instructions to keep the art on the denim after it dried and went through a wash cycle.
- MATH: Although this young student avoided math like the plague and had struggled with the subject, the math she needed to figure out for her painting project just came to her naturally, and she worked on the equations because she wanted to. She needed to figure out the ratios for her paint and thinner, the right sizes for her brushes, and the lengths of tape she used to measure off the area before painting the base. This was math on her grade level. Instead of straining to figure it out, she zipped through her equations so she could get started on her painting.

It was a full week of self-led curricula. When my writer friend saw what her daughter was able to accomplish—and how she created it on her own—she thought of imagination. She gave some serious thought to unschooling her child after school reopened post-quarantine. She ended up not doing so, primarily because she worried about socialization; while she could imagine unschooling, it was hard to imagine socializing her daughter in that construct. However, now she is working very hard on imagining unschooling her daughter while also finding a way to keep her socialized.

Deschooling and self-directed education have not been the subject of many peer-reviewed studies with large numbers. The studies that have been done, including informal surveys, have tended to lean toward positive experiences.

Whether it's your family structure, your gender or sexuality, your child's schooling or your livelihood, you can imagine something bigger than you realize. So can the people around you.

The Real World: In your regular day-to-day world, creating community and family will be something that you as an abolitionist will have to marinate on. A lot. Everything you do or say as it pertains to how you live your life will be put under a microscope. I have lived my life in many different ways, traditional and nontraditional. I've heard trolls try to say that how I live my life is the most dangerous element of my work.

If you're a single mom who chose to be a single mom, you're an abolitionist. If you're married for decades, you, too, are an abolitionist. If you identify as two-spirit and live blissfully in poly relationships where parenting is shared, you are an abolitionist. The point: create your families the way they work for you, whatever that looks like. Try your best to be as honest as you can about what you want and what you feel, because with this work as an abolitionist, you want your home to be a place of respite as much as it can be. You'll have to work at it, too, of course. But imagination is very important here. Imagine the structure you want—and build it.

GUIDING QUESTIONS

1. How do you use your imagination? Give a few examples of what you imagine about the most.
2. Name three things you will do to show up for your abolitionist imagination.
3. What are you most excited about when it comes to practicing imagination?
4. Are you scared or excited about your imagination? Why?

Forgive Actively, Not Passively

> The interpersonal work it takes to build community, to be comfortable and uncomfortable with each other, to learn how to come as our whole selves, to figure out how to hold space for all of these whole selves, to hold ourselves and each other accountable, to affirm and support each other, and enjoy each other's company takes time. It's a vital part and practice of working towards justice.
>
> —BadAss Visionary Healers

What does it mean to forgive actively vs. passively?

You're being demoted at work because of a careless mistake someone on your team made. Can you forgive, knowing that your entire household will be changed by this?

A friend has commented on your body in a way that is very offensive. Can you forgive? If you do, can you forgive passively or actively?

A driver, distracted, hits your car, causing damage and injuries. Can you forgive? If you do, can you forgive passively or actively?

A neighbor, speeding, hits and injures your pet.

Can you forgive? If you do, can you forgive actively or passively?

Your partner cheats on you. Can you forgive? If you do, can you forgive actively or passively?

Someone murders your loved one. Can you forgive? If you do, can you forgive actively or passively?

What if *you* were the person who did all these things? Would you want to be forgiven?

We tend to think of forgiveness as a singular thing, done in a singular way. Someone apologizes. You accept and forgive and move on. However, it's not quite that simple. Do you know where the person was coming from, what kind of hurt they may have been going through? Is it important? What frame of mind were you in during the grievance? Does that matter?

It all does.

Forgiving passively means you accept and forget. Forgiving actively means you become part of the process, even if it's uncomfortable.

Let's say a friend doesn't hold up their end of the bargain on a project. They apologize. You accept and move on. Except, it then happens again. Because you were passive with your forgiveness, you never got to a step where it was healed, not just scarred. The best apology comes with action. Forgiving someone actively comes with action steps. If you truly want to forgive someone, you want them to be better.

Forgiveness is rooted in the idea that we value each other and we are committed to each other's growth, healing and transformation. Forgiveness provides a pathway toward self-reflexiveness. When we persist in forgiveness we open up the space for the healing of our past and the healing of our future. As the BadAss Visionary Healers stated above, this is the bedrock of building community.

Forgiving actively gives the forgiver an agency that is often unmet when we hold on to what or who has harmed us. When we are unable to forgive or when we are hell-bent on holding on to a lack of forgiveness, we create a cycle of apathy at best, revenge at worst.

Unfortunately, so many of the tenets of forgiveness have been weaponized under a banner of religion or capitalism. My mother was disfellowshipped by the Jehovah's Witness religion she had belonged to. She (and her children) were shunned by the community. The culture dictated that no one in good standing could look her in the eye, shake her hand, offer her good tidings during services. She still attended services, hoping she would be forgiven. As is custom, she wrote a letter asking to be reinstated. The answer was *no*.

I watched this approach to forgiveness. Someone who believed, someone who tried, someone who gave their money and support. There was no forgiveness for imagined sins, passive or active. It made a distinct impression on me. I didn't want to be a part of any religion that treated its believers that way.

We are taught to forgive the person who committed horrific acts of harm against us and our community, and we are taught that the person who committed those harms doesn't have to be held accountable. We are taught a forgiveness that doesn't honor our own pain and hurt but focuses solely on the person who harmed us. In fact, forgiveness is often offered as a way to get out of accountability. The forgiveness I am calling for is a forgiveness that actually relies on an abolitionist praxis.

When we are in the forgiveness driver's seat, we begin to see that through forgiveness we are allowed to forge new roads that are paved with compassion, decisiveness and love. Forgiveness is not about cowardice or catering to our oppressors. An abolitionist's forgiveness identifies a move away from holding on to the toxicity of sorrow and victimhood. Abolitionist forgiveness becomes a pillar and tool we can use to create the healing conditions for our loved ones, as well as make demands for accountability for harm we have experienced. We also don't want to practice forgiveness prematurely. There have been times that I extended "forgiveness" in interpersonal relationships without the work that allows for forgiveness to be a seed that plants and grows new dynamics. In those instances, I recognized that the rush to forgiveness bred rotten roots of resentment. The work we do to forgive each other and ourselves has long-standing impacts on healing and growth. It provides the foundation for believing human beings can transform from the dominant toxic environment we all have ingested.

Forgiveness is a practice much like the other practices

in this book, it ebbs and flows. Forgiveness is not a race to be the most abolitionist. This is a patient road that pushes us to drive slowly because the impact of moving too quickly can cause major damage. Our forgiveness can take so many shapes. It can be something you have to actively work on every day in order to truly lean into the practice. Or forgiveness can be a practice that comes easily and with full grace and love. I have experienced forgiveness and its practice in a multitude of ways. As a young child I resented my mother. I was completely hurt and devastated that she didn't spend time with me, something I perceived as her inability to prioritize her children.

Through abolitionist forgiveness I realized my mother sacrificed her joys and her life to prioritize us solely. Not only was I able to forgive her but my bitterness transformed into compassion, and I was able to be a participant in a transformative dynamic between the both of us. Forgiveness pushes us toward each other. It makes us name where we are at in our dynamic and it opens up space for a continued healing journey.

Let's go back to one of the examples listed at the beginning of this chapter. You're being demoted at work because of a careless mistake someone on your team made. Can you forgive, knowing that your entire household will be changed by this? If your income and lifestyle are affected, how can you even passively forgive, much less actively? The truth is, you can. It's not easy. But you can. Talk it out in therapy. Talk it out with your circle. Write out how active forgiveness can keep you healthy and whole. Think about how this demotion could lead to better opportunities. There are always better things when we (try!) active forgiveness.

What to Read/Watch/See/Hear: Beyoncé's *Lemonade*. I am not here to represent the Beyhive or make a call on how you feel about her status as an artist. *Lemonade*, her 2016 magnum opus, centers on stripping her marriage down to the bare bones, exposing it all, and then actively forgiving, with action steps involved. She says in the final song that she's found the truth beyond her partner's lies and that she'll trade her partner's broken wings for her own. It is art. It is her truth. It is one person's way of supporting active forgiveness.

What I Know: In chapter two, on reacting vs. responding, I shared an uncomfortable moment I had with my mom. It turned into an ugly argument, and we went several days without speaking to each other (and keep in mind, we live very close and usually speak a few times a day). After almost a week my mom reached out to me. She apologized. I apologized, too, and focused on forgiving actively and not passively. I didn't toss off an apology just because she did or so we could move on from the situation. That would be forgiving passively—and not in a way that would truly bring closure. As with all of our exercises, take a beat before acting. Does the person deserve forgiveness? Do you deserve forgiveness from this person? Are there courageous conversations that need to be had first?

My mom reached out to me first. If she hadn't, I would have eventually reached out to her. Not to forgive or be forgiven. I would have asked her for a courageous conversation so we could discuss how we got there. Sometimes, forgiveness isn't even necessary. Sometimes, forgiving someone is a shortcut when what's really needed is a conversation about what happened. You can apologize and forgive and apologize and forgive and apologize and forgive over and over on the same topic. Sometimes, there needs to be an in-depth discussion or you'll be in a passive forgiveness loop forever.

Here's the other thing about forgiveness, both active and passive: sometimes, it's just not going to happen. There are times when the conflict just ends with conversation and moving on. I've been in situations where I had to actively forgive *myself* and not necessarily the other person involved.

I've had conflicts that ended with me thinking to myself, *Was I wrong? Should I apologize? Should I ask for active forgiveness?* Sometimes, the answer to all three of these questions was *no*. Again, I'm human and so are you. You won't always be able to be the bigger person. I'm not even going to tell you I have some kind of magical method to be able to do that. Because it doesn't exist. You can try. Sometimes, the person you have to actively forgive in a scenario is yourself. Of course, if there's any place where you can see active forgiveness, try to accomplish it, for your own healing.

This is especially true in families, both your family of origin and the families we create. Learning to forgive actively makes us better abolitionists.

Over the years, I've had conflict with people who are no longer in my life. At least not actively. I do not wish them harm. I hold no grudges, and I want the best for them. I don't speak to these individuals nor do I bring them up in conversation with others. They exist—over there. I have forgiven them—over there. Nothing about them exists here, in my present.

For example, if a third party asked me to recommend someone for an opportunity and I know this once-upon-a-time person would be perfect for it, would I recommend them?

If I have forgiven them passively, I probably would not. This person hurt me. I've forgiven them, but that doesn't mean I'd present them with a positive opportunity. In all likelihood, that person I forgave passively probably wouldn't even cross my mind.

If I've done the work to forgive them actively, pushed the tough conversations with myself and them, talked out forgiveness with myself and them, I could get to a space where someone who once hurt me could still be someone I support.

Does it mean my relationship with the person would be the way it was before the conflict? Likely not. You can actively forgive from a distance if you need to stop a cycle of harm.

This is a skill I've worked on quite a bit, and I have made considerable progress. I know how to forgive passively and actively. I know when to forgive no one but myself (that one is rare, but it happens).

We're made to think that this abolitionist work needs to come from a place of anger, frustration and other intense emotions. For sure, that will sometimes be the case, but being an abolitionist requires a pure heart and a steady mind. That begins with being able to understand the natural ebb and flow of conflicts and strife. If you can't tell your brother or your cousin how you really feel about whatever went down, how can you actively forgive and move on when things get heated within your abolitionist family?

For as long as there have been abolitionists and like-minded organizations, there have been groups on the other side intent on dismantling progress, most times from within.

The best way to topple an organization (or a family, or a friendship, or a relationship) from the inside is to provoke the emotions that cause the most consternation and pain—jealousy, greed, pride, insecurity—and then just allow people to fall short of their goals or attack their comrades. All of these things can be dropped into a relationship and cause it to falter. What can help is active forgiveness. The conversations that lead to active forgiveness are the things that keep people in accord.

I'm not saying that abolitionist work means that you'll have your phones tapped and people will try to destroy your efforts from the inside out (I'm not *not* saying it, either).

What I *am* saying is that you can begin active forgiveness as a natural progression with courageous conversation, and you can likely heal any fissures, those that come from within or without.

Forgiving passively is getting a cut on your hand and noting that it's there and it doesn't hurt too much. Then moving on. The cut may heal just fine on its own, but there's also a good chance it won't heal well—and it will continue to be painful along the way. Forgiving actively is washing the wound, even though it won't feel pleasant. Forgiving actively is applying medication, even if it burns a bit. Forgiving actively is bandaging the cut although the bandage is not comfortable to wear. Forgiving actively is changing the bandages each day until the cut is healed. In this way, the end result is a fully healed cut with no scar. This is what we want for the conflicts in our bodies, as well.

Again, this is work. Again, this is practice. Forgive yourself (actively!) if you sometimes walk around with an internal cut rather than clean it and heal it.

What You Know: The best examples on forgiving actively have come from people I know and individuals I have met through my lectures and travels who have shared their stories with me. That especially applies to forgiving actively. Ava, a friend I've spoken with about the act of forgiving actively, experienced a friend breakup that was tough to get over. There were unkind words lobbed in both directions. Months later, there was still vitriol. Ava was owed money for a broken lease for the apartment they shared. Her former friend felt that there was an error in the calculations and that they were even financially. There was a shared pet that now lived with Ava and had past-due veterinary bills that she believed should be shared. It went on and on this way. Ava had a grievance, her friend had an equally important one. It continued, round and round, with no progress made. It actually got worse. The police were called when Ava tried to retrieve some items that belonged to her. They both landed in small claims court over some minor belongings. It ramped up higher and higher. Eventually, they petered out. No one apologized to the other. Ava's former friend moved cross-country and eventually fell out of contact.

Ava was left with an unhealed wound, no bandage, no medicine. How could it have been different?

There's an expression in business management: begin with the end in mind. Which simply means, start with what you want. Not how you're getting there. Looking back, for Ava, what did she actually want? Not what did she want from her friend? What did she want, period?

Did she really want the money for the security deposit or the vet bills? She actually didn't need it for either. It was more about the anger about the end of the relationship. The time and effort she spent arguing, fighting, and in court was not about the material things. It was about the lack of transparency, the lies, the anger and the hurt.

What if Ava and her friend had been able to sit down for a conversation that could have led to active forgiveness? What if they could have put everything on the table, all the ugliness, all the cuts, and found a way to heal together and actively forgive?

Sometimes, the art of active forgiveness means sacrificing what is upsetting, whether it's an argument, an amount of money or a rumor of some sort. Get to the underbelly of what's keeping you from healing the wound.

Through her own work, particularly in therapy, Ava made her amends to herself and actively forgave her friend in absentia.

Remember, you will often have to forgive yourself, actively, before you can forgive anyone else. In our communities, we often have secrets and shameful situations that we have to deal with. These moments follow us into any abolitionist work we strive to do. So before (or while) we take on the heavy challenge of dismantling white supremacy, let's make sure we can ask Mom for a courageous conversation and some active forgiveness when she works our nerve—or when we work hers.

Those Who Can Show: John Lewis was born near Troy, Alabama, on February 21, 1940. His parents, Eddie and Willie Mae Lewis, were sharecroppers, and Lewis was one of ten children helping to tend the land and animals. Lewis's humble beginnings would greatly impact his political beliefs about morality and principles, which would eventually lead to his designation as the "conscience of Congress." In his autobiography in graphic novel form, *March*, he describes how he had wanted to be a preacher as a child and would often practice his sermons on the chickens. This steadfast dream to be aligned with all things fair and righteous followed him into adulthood as he became hyperaware that even after the 1954 *Brown v. Board of Education* decision, nothing much changed in his rural community, where schools remained segregated.

Lewis enrolled at Fisk University and was among the students who organized sit-in demonstrations at segregated lunch counters in Nashville, Tennessee. In 1961, he took that work a step further and participated in the Freedom Rides, challenging segregation at interstate bus terminals across the Jim Crow South. Oftentimes, Freedom Riders, with their nonviolent tactics, were met with great violence from angry mobs, including the Ku Klux Klan, or were beaten into compliance and arrested by police officers.

Lewis's leadership was recognized very early on when he was named chairman of the Student Nonviolent Coordinating Committee (SNCC) from 1963 to 1966 at the height of the Civil Rights Movement. His commitment to nonviolence solidified and was exemplary during the historic 1963 March on Washington, where he worked closely with leaders like Rosa Parks, Martin Luther King Jr. and Roy Wilkins (to name a few) to abolish the institutionalized discrimination that was so rampant in the South. His fiery speech that day called upon the soul of the nation to challenge the government's request to trust the bureaucracy: "To those who have said 'Be patient and wait,' we must say that 'patience' is a dirty and nasty word. We cannot be patient; we do not want to be free gradually. We want our freedom, *and we want it now.*"

On Sunday, March 7, 1965, 600 nonviolent protesters gathered at Selma's Edmund Pettus Bridge to begin a 50-mile march to the Alabama State Capitol in Montgomery. The march's focus was to protest the disenfranchisement of Black people from the electoral process. Lewis, the youngest of the "Big Six" Civil Rights activists who were leading the nonviolent march, was one of the first to be brutalized by state and local police when they attacked with billy clubs and tear gas. Lewis suffered a fractured skull and, despite the injuries, remained pacifist during the attacks. The march was televised, so millions of people across the nation witnessed the cruelty, and it successfully moved the moral compass needle of Congress. Five months after the march, President Lyndon Johnson signed the Voting Rights Act into law, demonstrating that nonviolent direct action was, in fact, effective.

Lewis carried his commitment to the philosophy of

nonviolence and steadfast views of justice equally; they were pillars that he honored during his lifetime. Not many people in Congress can say that they stood in the trenches to fight for the dignity and respect of oppressed people, but Lewis did just that. In fact, he was arrested 40 times in the 1960s, and while serving in Congress he was arrested a handful of times for protesting against the South African apartheid regime as well as against violence in Sudan and U.S. immigration policies. He recounted that even while held captive in jails, he made the conscious decision to be kind to the prison guards and held no contempt toward the police officers who brutalized him.

He actively forgave the very people who wronged him because "[t]hat's what the movement was always about, to have the capacity to forgive and move toward reconciliation." Lewis's most powerful trait was his ability to forgive and his belief in people's capacity to learn and to grow. The most well-known example of his mercy is the "apology heard 'round the world," when Lewis met with Elwin Wilson, who was among the men who had assaulted Lewis during the Freedom Rides of 1961. In 2009, Wilson had a realization and traveled to Washington to seek forgiveness for his violent acts. Lewis accepted his apology and met with Wilson to have a heartfelt conversation. Wilson recounts his time with Lewis as a meaningful moment in his life.

The power of his grace exemplified a well-earned moral authority that modeled for the nation how we, too, could take part in transforming the world by first transforming ourselves. Lewis invited people to create a new set of relationships and attitudes that required that we acknowledge our humanity above all. His enduring strength, courage and tenacity for justice inspired generations to "[b]e hopeful" and to "[n]ever, ever be afraid to make some noise and get in good trouble, necessary trouble." Lewis is memorialized as a long-standing, powerful leader and fulcrum of change in the United States.

How We'll Grow: We practice forgiveness because the shape of white supremacist patriarchy is about punishing ourselves and each other when we feel harmed. The system of punishment orients itself around an enemy that is not only unforgivable but unlovable and untransformable. So we practice to center love and transformation.

We practice forgiveness so we can deepen our commitment to a transformed self, collective and world. We deepen our faith in humanity when we center forgiveness and we create narratives that are rooted in trust and honesty vs. distrust and suspicion. I grew up in a community largely pushed out and punished by laws that were created to keep us at the margins. If your own government does not trust you and is hell-bent on attacking and undermining you, this has grave consequences emotionally. When I feel emotionally unsafe or vulnerable, it is more difficult for me to show up fully for my people.

We practice so the communities we live in can undo the burden of personal failure and understand that so much of what has failed us is the system, not ourselves. We practice forgiveness so we can take back our own humanity.

Cancel culture has produced dangerous environments for young people. I am much more interested in forgiveness culture. How, who and why we forgive tells us a lot about what our future lives can potentially be like.

Can you think of someone, right now, that you are at odds with? You don't need to necessarily approach them, but think of what forgiveness would look like. Could you forgive them at all, even passively? Is there space to work on forgiving them actively? What would that look like? Ask a friend or someone you trust to share with you a situation where it was difficult to actively forgive someone. Based on your readings, what do you see? Is this situation, based on what you now know, worthy of active forgiveness? Should it be left alone entirely? Talk it out as much as both of you feel comfortable doing.

The Real World: In the real world, you can't forgive actively or passively if you're not taking care of yourself. So, I was asked if I would talk about the practice of self-care in this book. I rolled my eyes as hard as I could. Honestly, I don't like the term "self-care." I know that Black feminist thought developed the concept as a revolutionary principle. I know that Audre Lorde famously said that self-care is a radical and political act. Which it is. However, it's also a little bubble-filled-tub sticker that comes with your planner. It's also used ironically: that third glass of wine is self-care, people say with a wink.

All those things may very well work for you (most of them work for me!). However, the actual terminology has been co-opted and watered down. Yes, take care of yourself. It's really not just for self. It's for everyone. Let's just call it caring for yourself.

Yes, caring for yourself, whatever that looks like, builds the foundation for you to show up with the capacity to actively forgive. Pretty much everything you do in abolitionist work will be dependent on caring for yourself.

GUIDING QUESTIONS

1. Is there someone in your life you want to forgive, but you don't know how to?
2. What do you understand about forgiveness and its role in your community and family?
3. What is hard about forgiveness?
4. Is there someone you need to ask for forgiveness? If so, who? Why?
5. Write out how you plan on practicing this principle.

Allow Yourself to Feel

Pain is important: How we evade it, how we succumb,
how we deal with it, how we transcend it.
—Audre Lorde, *Conversations with Audre Lorde*

Those who seek to work in the world of abolition likely come from a world designed to numb feelings.

Many of us grow up exposed to hurtful experiences. If we don't manage them and process them, we may disconnect from ourselves and each other completely and not feel our past, present or future. You may get through each day, you may even accomplish what you need to do. The truth of the matter is that you likely have generations of hurt that you're numbing to get through each day. In *Conversations with Audre Lorde*, the activist and poet talks about her outsider status—even as she worked tirelessly for Black women externally. Her otherness was often painful and, she said, "necessary."

Feelings from joy to sadness are essential for development and growth. You can't make progress if you only allow yourself to process positive feelings. You can't make progress if you only allow yourself to process negative feelings. Sorting them properly and honestly and having a plan in place to deal with them is non-negotiable. It's non-negotiable for anyone—doubly so if you plan to do abolitionist work.

The white supremacist capitalist patriarchy is designed and held in place with trauma. From enslavement to the activity of the Klan to the movements of the police, it's all about taunting and terrorizing, daring the people it's keeping down to react violently. We've taught ourselves, our children and our communities how to not feel (and for good reason). In many instances, it's the only way to survive. We have fear. We hold on to that like a security blanket. But other emotions? Like, love, anger, rage, disappointment, excitement? We're taught to be led by fear and keep all other emotions bottled up.

For many of us, it was manifested in childhood in idioms like: *fix your face* or *you better stop crying before I give you something to cry about.* Think about this. A child, usually younger than a teenager, is being physically beaten. Like any human being, the reaction to that is crying or some other fear-based reaction. The counter-response, usually from adults, is to tell the child not to show that fear or pain or frustration—*or they'll get more of the punishment.*

Of course, if that is your upbringing, you'll learn to numb out, to not feel feelings. You'll learn to numb that part of you that is vulnerable. You'll tuck it away and no one will be able to get to it—including yourself.

Here's where things start to fall apart. What help is

our movement work if you can't feel the impact of the trauma or the joy? How do you help your fellow comrades if you can't feel? How do you work with people whose communities and families have been decimated by white supremacy, who have been numbed—if you haven't handled how it's affected you and your family?

Consider this: so many of us have had *that* relative. It's an elder, of any gender, who doesn't easily communicate with their partner or children or families. At a family gathering, they are silent, perhaps speaking solely to chide someone or complain. They don't seem to have any emotions except annoyance. Whether it's a graduation, wedding, funeral or holiday, they don't have much to say. You can't ask about the family tree, you can't ask about the good old days or family recipes. These are the family members who are surviving the impact their trauma has had on them. Sitting on the tweed couch with plastic slipcovers with not much to say.

We know why this is. It's because so many of our elders have had to bind up their emotions tight, like a bandaged rib, for their entire lives. Any emotion, positive or negative, was blunted over the years while they just tried to survive.

We can do better. We owe it to them to do better—or at least to try. It is not easy. It's a practice that endures. It's worth it. Sucking up emotions is partly why our life expectancy is much lower than it should be.

Feelings are important because they help us identify our hurts and joys. They help us understand our emotional makeup, thus giving us more possibility and range in naming our needs. Black and poor people in particular are often told directly or indirectly that our feelings do not matter and thus our needs do not matter.

We are taught to stuff all the terrible shit that happens to us down in dark corners of our souls. We are trained to just "take it" and that the feelings we have bear no weight because our bodies, spirits, hurt and joy don't matter. Stuffing our feelings or not acknowledging them creates a cycle of self-blame and self-harm that in fact impacts every part of our lives.

As abolitionists the goal of allowing ourselves to feel gives us agency to be the dynamic human beings that we actually are. When we can locate our feelings and give clear and nuanced voice to them, we provide a new pathway for processing our feelings. We also get to identify what the feelings are expressing and what we need from ourselves and others.

When I was a child, I was told that I was too sensitive. I cried easily, felt joy often and wore my heart on my sleeve. I didn't have good examples of how to hold space for my feelings, and that really created a lot of internal turmoil. If I could talk to my younger self right now, I'd tell her, *It's okay to feel. Hold on to it.*

I'd tell her that her big feelings are a superpower and if harnessed responsibly can provide deep healing and understanding. As an abolitionist, I ask us to use our feelings as a first indicator of what we sense we like, love, feel uncomfortable with or are unhappy with. When we give ourselves permission to access our feelings, we can make decisions from a place that honors our needs and the needs of the community around us.

When we deny ourselves our feelings it is like denying ourselves water, food and basic sustenance. We need our emotional intelligence, because that brings us closer to abolition and liberation.

We owe it to our ancestors to feel. Feelings were a luxury for many of our forebears. It's literally a luxury to be sad, disappointed or upset. For people who lived under constant fear that their families could be dismantled at any time, to feel could be to lose your life.

On May 31 and June 1, 1921, in Tulsa, Oklahoma, a massacre was enacted on Greenwood, a Black neighborhood, leaving dozens dead and millions of dollars of property wiped out. It began when a Black teenager falsely accused of sexual assault was imprisoned. A group of armed Black men stood watch outside the jail to make sure the young man was not lynched. The group was asked to disperse, which they did. At some point, there was a scuffle with white men nearby. Someone's gun discharged. That was it—for the next 48 hours, there was loss of life and property.

But this is the true horror of that moment: Thousands of residents left Greenwood, and most of them never spoke about what happened over the course of those two days and why they left their entire lives behind. Those who remained never spoke a word of what happened. For generations. Most who lived through it took the stories, the atrocities, and the memories to their graves.

Try to really envision this: people are dead, homes are destroyed, and no one speaks out. No one demands justice. It is not discussed, even privately. It is folded up, placed deep inside the breast pocket of the community, white hot and painful. For decades, no one feels it because it's wrapped up so deep no one can even find it.

Those who come to abolitionist work are likely to come from a place of buried pain and feelings about things that could have manifested even before we were born.

The field of epigenetics is devoted to studying how trauma can be passed down to the next generation on a genetic level. While the work is still in its early stages, it does point to a direct genetic marker for people whose forbears experienced trauma like enslavement. They may have passed those feelings to their children and beyond. If this pain is literally in our genetic background, we must learn how to feel it and process it so we can heal from it and thus heal the next generation. If we can pass down trauma, then we can surely pass down healing.

This is another principle that is practiced best with professional help or within a community. Sometimes, it can get heavy. You want to be supported because what you discover in your work can be triggering for you or others.

What to Read/Watch/See/Hear: *The Body Is Not an Apology: The Power of Radical Self-Love* by Sonya Renee Taylor. Loving ourselves is a key way to help us learn the importance of feeling and healing. If you look into the mirror or touch yourself or see yourself in someone else's eyes—and love what you see and feel—it's the beginning of tapping into more positive emotions that will increase your strength for movement work.

What I Know: In 20 years of organizing, I've dealt with struggling to feel—too little and too much. As a young person, I watched older people put together all kinds of ways to not feel, including using one emotion (usually anger or rage) all the time; coping with drugs and alcohol, which can tamp feelings down; or just completely checking out and not letting anyone in, including themselves. Mental health matters here, too. If you have any sort of neurodivergent challenge and it's not being treated or maintained, being able to feel in a way that's constructive and helpful can be doubly hard to do. Sometimes, medications can be suggested to balance out these emotions, but if you depend on a medical system that is steeped in racism and white supremacy, you might not get the right care you need. Do your research on different healing methods and experiment to see what feels most aligned with your needs and values.

What You Know: Writer Aliya S. King shared with me that many years ago she read a haunting piece about what happens when people don't know how to process emotions properly. The writer described her grand-mother coming home ready to beat someone in the family for doing something wrong. It turned out that the child in question had not done anything wrong. Whatever the act was, she had not done it. Instead of letting it go, the grandmother said to all the children, "Well, I'm ready now. Someone's going to get this beat-ing. Which one of you is it going to be?" One of the sib-lings (who also was innocent) volunteered to take the beating. The rest of the sisters watched, silently.

How were those women affected by this? An elder who is determined to beat one of her children, even if they're all innocent? How does knowing your elder needs to do that affect you for the long haul? How does watching her actions affect you? When you've grown, and perhaps had that courageous conversation with your mom and your sisters and worked on active forgiveness, you'll still forever be affected by something like that.

In places like Tulsa and beyond, white supremacy has used the suppression of feelings to hold down com-munities. If you block the pain, you'll likely block the feelings needed to fight back against oppression.

We have to remember exactly how pain actually works. Pain is in our brain. If you touch a hot stove with your hand, you'll feel a jolt of pain. However, it's not your hand telling you that it hurts. Your nerves relay the message up to your brain and let you know: *This is hurting.*

Most of us don't have a problem identifying physical feelings: *this cut hurts, my back feels better, I have a headache,* a *stomachache.* We can identify what we feel on our bodies. What about elsewhere? Does your brain tell you when you're upset, confused, irate or low? How do you process that information? It's really important to figure this out if you want to be effective in your life as an abolitionist.

For the most part, we're all a bit better at feeling positive things than negative things. If we hear good news, we smile. If we see someone we've missed, we lean in for a hug. If we watch something that pulls at our heartstrings, we may cry. If we get a new job or leave a not-so-good job, we pump our fists with joy.

What about the other side of feeling? How do you process how it feels to lose a loved one? Do you try to grieve as quickly as possible so you can move on? Or do you let the grief go and work around it? Who has the right formula for how you feel difficult emotions? Only you do.

In Judaism, mourners who suffer a loss sit shiva for seven days, which means that the grieving stay at home, receive visitors and mourn. It's a set time to lean into the feelings that come with mourning. Whether you're completely devastated or only mildly sad, you have this seven-day period to allow yourself to feel. It's socially expected to take time and process. In various cultures, this period can go for as long as several months. In some cultures, it's literally looked upon strangely if someone doesn't wail and cry and show feelings over the death of a loved one.

Black and Brown folks have their own ways of dealing with grief depending on where they are from geographically and other markers. However, a wake, a service and a repast are common. The wake is usually offered in the evening, for those who can't attend the more formal funeral service, which ends with a large meal called a repast.

These things differ depending on who has passed away and what the circumstances were. The older the person who has passed and the more expected the passing, the more likely there will be traditional markers.

But we usually have a grieving process. The year 2020, with a completely different program, threw this into disarray. Funerals were on Zoom, with fewer than five people in person, standing six feet apart, in masks. It made it even harder for us to process grief.

When your mom passes away alone, in an ICU, with no visitors, that will affect how you handle grief.

It's not just death; something like a minor disagreement with a friend or a loved one can send that signal to your brain: *we feel*. It's up to you to determine how intense this feeling is and how long it should last.

It's been said to think of all of our feelings as a stew, forever bubbling in an old-school cauldron. The pot has to be continually stirred, over and over. That's the equivalent of checking in with ourselves. You would never leave a boiling dish on a stove indefinitely. Our brains are the same, and we constantly need to make sure they're not bubbling over.

We add feelings to this stew. We build connections. We grow our families. Keep stirring. We enter relationships. We become abolitionists. We change laws. We dismantle systems of oppression. Keep stirring. At no point do you ever just walk away from this pot filled with all your feelings. You will always make sure everything is simmering at the right temperature. Sometimes, you'll take things out. The way we scoop out a bay leaf at the end of making spaghetti sauce. Some things remain in there forever. What's important is that we measure what goes in and comes out. Keep stirring. Keep it all balanced.

Those Who Can Show: Prentis Hemphill is a healer and thought leader in our movement. He grew up in Arlington, Texas, with his mother and father and younger brother, Eddie Hemphill. He often talks about how being raised in the South shaped him as the human being he is today. Strong, often reserved, and one of the best dancers I know, Prentis is a Black trans healer from a red state and has been open about his decades-long battle with his own mental health. Perhaps that's why his work is so profound. You can tell with every group or person Prentis works with, he is deeply focused on their health and healing and ultimate well-being. He is a dear friend and comrade of mine, and he is also one of our best thinkers inside of this healing justice movement. Much of his work comes out of the Black radical tradition.

Prentis Hemphill is a movement facilitator, Somatics teacher and practitioner and writer living and working at the convergence of healing, individual and collective transformation and political organizing. He spent many years working with powerful movements and organizations, most recently as the Healing Justice director at Black Lives Matter Global Network. In 2016, Prentis was awarded the Buddhist Peace Fellowship Soma Award for community work inspired by Buddhist thought. Prentis is the founder of the Black Embodiment Initiative and host of the *Finding Our Way* podcast.

This podcast is a brilliant contribution to our abolitionist movement. It is through our conversations about embodiment that I deepened my own personal practice. Currently, Prentis teaches with Black Organizing for Leadership and Dignity, a training program for Black organizers throughout the United States, and works as a facilitator and consultant for organizations and groups looking to center healing justice and transformative justice into the very core of their work to build more well and self-determined communities.

Prentis has served as a board member for the National Queer and Trans Therapists of Color Network (NQTTCN), a network for connecting communities with representative mental health practitioners and an effort to bring sound frameworks of healing justice into current mental health provision models.

Prentis is also a deeply committed practitioner and healer who utilizes Somatics methodology, an intuitive and ancestral practice, in his work to heal trauma and unlock the unique brilliance and contribution of each person, body and being they work with. During his time as Healing Justice director at Black Lives Matter, he became the go-to person for intrapersonal conflict inside of the organization. Prentis always prioritized the feelings and emotions that came up for the folks inside of the organization. There wasn't a single time I felt like he was bulldozing through what was most painful or challenging for all people involved. Prentis's work is about showing up for ourselves and our deepest longings and desires.

How We'll Grow: I know, I know. You're done with opening that notebook and getting ready to take notes on how to make that principle come to life. This one is super easy. Let's create a hypothetical mental cauldron for an abolitionist. Call it "How to Feel." Imagine that's what it says on your ever-boiling pot. What's in there? Your meetings never start on time. Throw some *impatience* in that pot! Be careful! It can burn if you don't tend to it. What else is in there? Perhaps some of your fellow abolitionists have more formal education than you do? Go ahead and throw that feeling of *insecurity* in there. It's bitter, right? Go ahead and taste it and understand it may always be there in some form, right at the center of your stew. Has it been months doing abolitionist work with no rest in sight? There's *exhaustion*, right on the top. You can skim that off occasionally and replenish yourself regularly.

As you continually tend to your stew, jot down all the feelings that come through in a given day: annoyance, frustration, joy, grief, bitterness, fear. You'll be surprised just how many feelings you have throughout the day. If we don't really think about it, most of us assume we're automatons, just getting work done, eating a meal and then going to bed every night. We're so much more complex than that. If you don't even recognize what you're feeling each day, you likely aren't feeling it properly. Or at all.

This is not pleasant. Imagine leaving the house not knowing what you are wearing—or if you're wearing anything at all. Imagine leaving the house not knowing how your hair was styled. Imagine leaving the house not knowing if you have your keys, your wallet and your phone.

These are things that are second nature to us. We check and double check them, multiple times per day. We subconsciously reach for those things throughout the day. Do we reach for where we are in our feelings? If not regularly, then daily? Weekly? It's likely we don't. You can't be more in tune with where your backpack is than where your feelings are. Check in. Stir the pot. Look for where you are.

Remember what white supremacy is. It's the belief that white people are superior and that they should dominate. This has been sustained with many different methods, abject fear and terror among them. It feels as if we can't overcome things like white supremacy. So it's important that we figure out how to put those feelings to work. Abolishing white supremacy and the patriarchy depends on not necessarily controlling your feelings but understanding them and knowing when and how to expect them. If you have feelings of rage because of things you see in your work as an abolitionist, how can you make sure you process them properly if you don't know how to process joy or simple annoyance? If it's in the stew, it needs to be properly handled if you want to be able to go out and handle the bigger stuff.

Bracketing your feelings also helps you understand how white supremacy and patriarchy work. This work will not always bring feelings of joy or peacefulness. You have to be able to identify, process and move on. You are literally fighting for the right to exist. You are fighting for the right to emote. You are fighting for the right to speak up for what is needed in our communities.

You have to be able to feel in order to get others to understand why you *should* be able to feel. When you can feel free, you can feel.

Leadership is an essential part of movement work; we need to make sure we have strong people, at home, at work, wherever you have to show up, being present and leaning into what you feel.

Abolitionists must have the fullness that comes with true feelings. This isn't simple work. If you need counsel to deal with how you handle emotions, seek it. Remember that you're not just doing it for yourself. You're doing it for your community and for the movement at large.

The Real World: For femme people in a patriarchal society, this is an especially important principle. We are often raised to *nurture, nurture, nurture* others. Often, as the saying goes, mothers raise their daughters and love their sons. Somehow, we expect girls to be women without ever having been girls. A young girl will be expected to care for her siblings and do chores around the house while a brother, even older, might not. It's a legacy that's been carried down for many years, and we actively need to teach femme people that their feelings need to be honored and respected—for the entirety of their upbringing and femmehood. They also need the skills, including self-defense, proper education and self-sufficiency, to be able to process feelings that are specific to their lives.

When I was younger and took the bus everywhere, I had a ritual I created for whenever I needed to walk home alone at night: (1) Make sure to wear something baggy; (2) don't look anyone in the eyes; (3) the minute you get off of the bus, RUN!; (4) stay off the sidewalk and always stay in the middle of the street.

I would also recite the steps my father taught me on how to defend myself if a man tried to kidnap me. I spent a lot of my youth reciting my survival tools. Women and femmes need to be taught to protect themselves because they are in constant imminent danger. This shapes how we see the world and how we see ourselves.

Feelings are developed in individual moments that are taught to us early on. We must work at making space for acknowledging them and being present for the impact they have on our lives.

GUIDING QUESTIONS

1. In what aspects of your life do you try *not* to feel?
2. What's the scariest part about allowing yourself to feel?
3. When was the last time you felt deeply about something? Was it a positive or negative experience?
4. How can feeling deeply connect to abolitionist practice and dismantling white supremacy?

Commit to Not Harming or Abusing Others

Our movements themselves have to be healing, or there's no point to them.
—Cara Page, Kindred Southern Healing Justice Collective

It seems simple, right? We are not walking around this world thinking of harming or abusing others. I'm talking about *committing* to not harming or abusing others. How do we do this? How can you be intentional about it? We often assume we won't hurt others, then apologize if we do and move on. In her conversations with the Southern Healing Justice Collective, Cara Page talks about centering generational trauma and oppression in her work.

However, committing to anything is an action step, and action steps take bravery and intention. You can never just assume you won't harm someone. So consider this chapter to be car insurance. No, you don't want to have to use it. But if you don't have it when you need it, the fallout will be a lot worse.

Violence doesn't happen in a vacuum. It is connected to the conditions that we live in, and we all participate in creating those conditions, and we all have a collective responsibility for ending violence, harm and abuse.

This makes people uncomfortable. I'm not responsible for violence! Why do I have a collective responsibility for ending violence, harm and abuse? The answer is simple: You are a decent human being and you live in a world where we all need to perpetuate an anti-harm environment.

Let's continue our car insurance example. On a highway a driver rear-ends the car in front of them. That car hits another. The car behind hits the first car. There is damage to several cars although just one person is at fault. If the first driver has car insurance, everyone else will be taken care of. What if this first driver doesn't have car insurance? It's a different situation now. Everyone needs to have car insurance for the greater good of everyone on the highway. What we do and don't do impacts others. If one person doesn't have car insurance and they get in a multi-car accident, the entire driving community is impacted. Most importantly, someone needs to take accountability for it.

This principle may seem like a no-brainer. However, I want us to take a moment as human beings to realize that harm and abuse exist in multiple ways. We all have the capacity to *be* harmed and also have the capacity to *cause* harm. The sooner we are able to understand that the dichotomy of abuser and victim is inherently false, the closer we are to understanding how abolition can, will and does support moving all of us toward a healing path. Abuse is a reaction to the set of conditions we live inside of. The United States was built on harm and abuse. This country stole land through physical and sexual violence; it stole human beings and forced them to labor while labeling them as three-fifths human. It used violence and aggression to create a world of harm and greed.

We are a people whose teeth were stolen and used for dentures. Our hair was stolen and used to stuff furniture—along with the cotton we picked. We could go on for the rest of this book, itemizing the abuse and harm.

So, now, when you think of harming or abusing someone, you may think of physical abuse or physical fights and reactions to situations. Or any of the things mentioned above that were once regular forms of horrible behavior. Yes, that is harm and abuse, but what I'm talking about is more insidious than that.

The kind of generational trauma due to colonialism and its effects on human beings impacts every single human who lives in the world. That trauma provides an important framework for us to understand why abuse happens the way it does, especially in this country. Part of our commitment as abolitionists is to not harm or abuse people, especially *intentionally*.

Sometimes abuse and harm are done unintentionally, but whether we cause harm intentionally or unintentionally, it is our work to interrupt that pattern for the sake of healing and liberation. As a part of developing abolitionist spaces, collectives and institutions, we have to be careful to not enact the same harm and abuse we have been living and breathing in. That is why it is important that when we are creating new spaces, they are built as abolitionist spaces.

What is an abolitionist space? It's a place that practices safety. It's a place where all are intentional about not causing you harm. An abolitionist space is not always a physical meeting space for a large organization. Sometimes it's much more subtle than that, especially in the beginning. Sometimes it's a classroom. Sometimes it's a living room. Sometimes it's a break room. It's a place where you are cared for. Our goal is to be caring. That's what makes it a space to practice safety.

Are you caring to the people you work with in abolition? Do you understand why they may not be warm and caring to you? What are the small moments in your day-to-day life that matter and help you build and support safe spaces?

I have a friend, Lola, who recently hired an executive assistant. The young woman, Dani, was phenomenal and helped boost Lola's productivity within the first month. Dani was so good at scheduling and research that Lola could literally see her life mellowing out, and she was able to spend more time with her family and work on projects she was truly passionate about.

Lola always prided herself on being caring toward her employees and would go out of her way to make her office a safe, abolitionist place. She saw that Dani was going to have a bright place in her company, and she looked forward to mentoring her.

Then, something changed. Dani was not responding to emails, and she was making small errors on important documents. She scheduled meetings for the wrong time zone and other careless mistakes.

For one week, Lola noted the errors but didn't mention them. She knew she'd had weeks where she'd made many errors.

Then, the next week, more errors. Then the next week, more errors.

Lola knew that Dani was going to have to go. Other employees were now being affected by her mistakes, and it just wasn't working. Before that, however, she tried to think intentionally about it. Lola had a feeling that letting Dani go was going to be harmful to this young woman. Whatever was going on, getting fired was not going to help her.

Lola called Dani and asked her, plainly, what was going on. Dani apologized and explained. It was the anniversary of a very traumatic event in her life, and she hadn't realized it would affect her so strongly.

Lola felt for Dani, but she also knew she had an entire company to run and needed it done properly. Yet, she decided that her assistant was worth helping. She told Dani to take a full week off. She could have some time to clear her mind and rest. Then, if she was up to it, she could return.

For that week, my friend was a bit frazzled and got a temp to cover some of the bases. Her employees were again frazzled with less help, but she asked them to be patient and gave extensions to pertinent projects.

When Dani returned, Lola felt like she had done the right thing. Her assistant has been superb ever since, and it only cost Lola a week of minor inconvenience. She needed Dani to feel seen, and she needed the rest of her employees to see the way their team operated. Ultimately, the entire experience made her work environment feel like a healthy space for the folks working with each other. Having a bad week (or even three) would not be an immediate reason to be fired. First, you needed to be treated like a human.

People are not bots. They are human, and if we're going to work on feeling our feelings, we have to urge others to do the same. Dani now knows that she can tell Lola that she's in need. That's powerful.

In many cultures, spankings and beatings have been used as discipline and punishment for millennia. Some kids have been forced to kneel on rice, sometimes while holding a heavy load on their head. Some have endured beatings with belts, switches (that they were forced to find), shoes and extension cords. Some have been slapped, choked and screamed at.

Today, many of us laugh at this trauma. Stand-up

comedians and movies make jokes about the good old days.

Even without physical punishment, we feared our parents. We feared getting our "good" clothes dirty. We feared saying anything or touching anything if we went into a store. We feared what would happen if we spoke up for ourselves. If we talked back. If we even made a face that wasn't acceptable. Some of us lived that kind of built-in terror all the time.

We know now. It was abuse. Pure and simple. Whether we have now (actively) forgiven the people who raised us or not—we know now it was abuse.

Some of us got the same form of abuse we see in white supremacy from our relatives, while our humanity was still being formed. Then we were doubly harmed when the white supremacist patriarchy took hold as we got older.

We must remember, whether we forgive or not, corporal punishment was a survival tactic from our ancestors. Keeping your child quiet, by any means necessary, was literally often needed to stay alive. Using nothing but a stare to make sure your children stay completely silent has also been just a normative part of parenting. Many of us have stories to tell about going to markets and stores with our parents and seeing white children acting *out* in ways that would bring us bodily harm if we were to try the same behavior with our own parents.

Our parents thought they had to harm us in order to make us listen to them—so they could keep us safe.

Many of us were *trained* with violence to listen and to obey.

We were harmed. We must decide to passively forgive, actively forgive or do neither. We must remember where the abuse came from.

We must commit to not harming and abusing others. If necessary and possible, we have to let go of what harm and abuse influenced us in order to make sure we don't do it again.

Certain harms and abuses are still frighteningly common in our communities. (And worldwide. The United Kingdom is currently making it illegal to hit your child under any circumstance.)

There has been very strong evidence against spanking, and it's known to be both harmful and abusive. It makes children more aggressive. Many parents know they can use words instead of physical actions to get the behavior they want from their children. So why is it that nearly half of all American parents still support spanking? Why is it still something to joke about? Why still the talk about *chanclas* and switches?

I know firsthand that it's just not worth it. In my household, like many, it was a multigenerational life, and I helped to raise my nephew. He'd been removed from both of his parents. Eventually, my mom gained full custody of him, and we all had to be conscious and intentional about how we were going to raise him. Very early on, I made a vow to never hit him. Not a slight pop or anything else. Just no hitting. Period. I made it clear to all of our other family members: do not put your hands on this boy.

Many times, kids get spanked not because of what they did but because of what the adult was feeling at the time it was done. When parents are on edge, nervous, exhausted, it can lead to spanking their child instead of having a conversation.

What we had to lean on and really help my nephew with: use your voice and your words.

Once he saw that we would listen and act when he used his words instead of lashing out, we all started to find our way. It didn't necessarily get easier, but it did get clearer.

Almost immediately, and throughout his childhood, I saw a huge difference between a spanking and a non-spanking home. I saw the instances where I would have been hit and how much easier it was to choose another option. Again, I've made my peace with how I was parented, but I'm also grateful I got to see it done differently with my nephew.

What some parents really want is for their children to have that abject fear of them; but that only means kids do things in secret and are afraid to ask for help. Making the decision not to spank is not an easy one, especially when it's been an approved and accepted and expected part of parenting in your culture for generations.

I want my nephew and all Black children to stand up tall and walk this earth like they mean it. If they cower in fear of their parents, instead of contributing to being parented, they will cower in fear of all authority while defying it, as well.

If we're abolitionists and we're fighting to not be harmed and abused by the white supremacist patriarchal structure, we have to make sure we're not harming or abusing, either. We have to take it very seriously.

So, cause no harm. Cause no abuse. Also, understand where it comes from if you do.

Be honest, do you ever gossip about your friends or frenemies? Do you sometimes use social media to cut down someone else's hair, clothes, relationship, career? Can you be judgmental about the choices your friends and family make? Just because you're not critical to someone's face doesn't mean you're not causing harm. In fact, if you're whispering behind your hand to someone else, you're giving off negativity to them as well, which is another way of causing harm.

We're human. There's so much about our everyday life that could be considered causing harm. Like we just discussed, we all have feelings we try to adjust to on a daily basis, and we're by no means perfect. You could be cross with your child because you're just exhausted. You could set unreasonably high expectations for your partners and then not be kind when they can't measure up. Your puppy could be taking too long to get the hang of Wee-Wee pads. A parent could be making you feel guilty for not calling more. Whatever our interactions are with the people in our lives, we need to be sure that our reactions are not harmful or abusive.

Life is about challenges. How you handle them is about who you are and how you show up to your practice. Your reactions and responses are paramount.

I know a mom whose 13-year-old can be challenging. She's not completing all of her homework assignments and chores. The mom took her phone away as a punishment, which made the child's attitude even worse. Is there harm or abuse happening here? Is the teen, who often exhibits challenging behavior, actually harming her mom? Or is there something missing in the relationship that's causing the disconnect? This mom goes out into the world on a daily basis to fight against a white supremacist system. Yet, some days, the fight is even harder than it should be because of the fights she's having at home.

Harm and abuse are not always easy to spot, gauge or avoid. We simply do our best. You must always be ready to put into practice active forgiveness, when possible, including and especially for yourself.

What to Read/Watch/See/Hear: *Hood Feminism* by Mikki Kendall. This book examines how society and our power structure, including capitalism, racism, white supremacy and patriarchy, affect Black women.

What I Know: My brother Monte was diagnosed with schizoaffective disorder while he was incarcerated because of, and during, an episode. Instead of receiving medical care, my brother was beaten, chained to a bed, and became severely emaciated. I was heartbroken and angry.

Monte is one young Black man among hundreds of thousands who have similar stories. They end up in the prison system, they are tortured, they are separated from their families, they are nowhere near rehabilitated (many didn't need rehabilitating in the first place).

It doesn't just affect Monte and all the young men like him in this country, it affects the mothers, like my own, the sisters, like me and my sister. This harm and abuse settles over a family like a fine layer of sand that's impossible to filter out. It grates. It grinds. It causes friction that spreads. It's more than just harm and abuse, it's a cancer.

Leah Lakshmi Piepzna-Samarasinha, an activist whose work is both far-reaching and healing, has developed insight and contributions to disability justice, specifically when speaking on neurodivergent, sick and disabled people. They elevated my understanding of the complexities of harm and abuse and our responsibility to forge healing systems collaboratively.

Healing is a rigorous practice that can only be effectively done at what Leah calls the "speed of trust." To commit to not harming or abusing others means that we are taking a closer look at the larger structures of violence that we have survived and all the ways we have internalized that violence.

Many of us have survived. Many of us have even

thrived. Whenever anyone asks why my life as an activist exists, I tell them simply: my brother Monte. I was up close to my brother's harm and abuse. I knew what he and many like him actually needed. I love my brother very much and seeing the way he was treated just turned on my switch. I was going to work on his behalf and on behalf of all the other Montes.

The disability and transformative justice framework asks us to consider the intersection of ableism and racism and how survivors are criminalized and pathologized. Disability is oftentimes erased and depoliticized, but this is dangerous because it leaves this population vulnerable to the criminal legal system, especially for neurodivergent folks. As we grapple with the recent uprisings to defend Black lives and end the prison/police state, we cannot ignore that one-third to one-half of all people murdered by police are disabled and/or deaf people or have mental health issues.

That singular statistic should be enough to have people gather around statehouses and legislative bodies to demand justice. If not that, we should be gathering around each other and demanding justice. Those most in need of care are the most likely to not receive it.

There has been much data compiled that outlines the ways in which Black disabled people are disproportionately impacted by state violence. As we commit to reducing harm and abuse, we need to consider the types of interventions we have for neurodivergent people that do not solely rely on the police or institutionalization. Leah is challenging able-bodied people to be accomplices to disabled folks and think through other possibilities for intervention and access that reduce the harm and violence people experience. It will not be a perfect process. It will require us to have really honest conversations about power dynamics and privilege, and these hard conversations and change will not happen overnight.

But the treatment of Black disabled people has to change. We can't be afraid to call for help when a loved one needs support. We can't have a system that uses the prison system to address neurodivergent issues. We can't have authorities that are being trained with the same ineffective methods that were used at the turn of the twentieth century.

We can't keep losing our children, parents and loved ones this way. It's not humane and it's not right, in the most primal of ways. I am committed to change.

In the case of neurodivergent people experiencing emotional crisis, these intentional conversations have to be centered around each person's agency and not the able-bodied person's savior tendency and desire to "fix" people. We have to take the time to be responsive and ask about triggers, trauma responses and consent as we build a safety and wellness plan for people experiencing an emotional crisis. Able-bodied people cannot assume we know "what's best"—it is harmful to strip people of their right to self-determination. When we co-create life-saving and life-giving plans, we are creating an infrastructure that can be truly liberatory and healing for all people involved.

All of our abolitionist systems have something in common: the answers are within us. Whether we have an advanced degree in sociology and prison reform or we just have seen a family member harmed, we can challenge this system to do better.

Mental health challenges of all kinds are a serious source of harm and abuse for our people, and we often live a life filled with more harm than help. Within our families, we often either don't talk about mental health or sweep it under the rug if it does come up.

It's mostly because so many of us just don't understand much of it. The terminology, the options, the medications, the therapists, the diagnoses—it can all be confusing, expensive and terrifying. Sometimes we just don't want to confront it.

And we have a reason to not always confront it. We don't have the freedom to have a tough moment in our health. If we are upset, crying, screaming, hard to understand, maybe even damaging property or threatening to harm ourselves or others, that can be a death sentence. If the police are called on someone in that state, there's a great chance that the care they will receive is a bullet or a Taser.

In 1984, Eleanor Bumpurs was set to be evicted from her New York City apartment because she was several months behind in her rent. After several visits from social workers, it was determined that she needed to be hospitalized for several mental health issues.

Somehow, it was decided that Eleanor Bumpurs would be evicted from her apartment *before* receiving the medical care she urgently needed. There was a program in place for people to get emergency grants to cover back rent in situations like this. For some reason, this was never done. The social worker assigned to her case thought it made sense for a 66-year-old woman who was hallucinating to be forced out of her apartment and then perhaps admitted to a hospital.

She was failed by so many departments. The housing authority, the social workers, even the maintenance crew.

Now, Bumpurs needed help. She was walking around her apartment with a ten-inch knife. She was threatening and had bottles of feces in her tub. She was consistently yelling about Ronald Reagan and saying that people were out to get her.

Bumpurs needed to be kept safe for herself and for others. This is fact. But that is not what happened. When someone is paranoid and hiding in their apartment to avoid getting evicted, you do not send six officers to her apartment to put her out.

Bumpurs was indeed admitted to the hospital just two hours after eviction proceedings began. But it wasn't so that she could receive care. She had been shot and killed by one of the six police officers who forced their way into her home after she refused to let anyone in.

The officer was at first charged in Bumpurs's death.

He was ultimately acquitted. The judge said he did what he was supposed to do. After an appeal, charges were brought against the officer again. At trial, he was acquitted.

The city of New York failed Eleanor Bumpurs. She had paid her rent on time for years (it was $89), and just a few months after falling behind and not being in the right mind to handle it—she was dead.

This is harm. This is abuse. This is what we're fighting against. We're fighting for the Eleanor Bumpurses of the world. We're fighting for the Montes of the world. We're fighting for ourselves.

We need a multi-layered approach. We have to constantly stir that cauldron and sift it for harm and abuse done toward us, and we have to constantly work to curb the harm and abuse that is a constant.

Abolitionist work could be called *Reduce Harm and Abuse* because essentially white supremacy is harmful and abusive and uses that harm and abuse to maintain itself.

Here's what I know. We have to look around ourselves on a regular basis and see how our smallest actions can stop harm and abuse. What kind of language are we using with and about our comrades?

Of course, we also have to think about how we're harming and abusing ourselves.

How are you caring for yourself? Are you seeing doctors regularly? Are you doing the research necessary to make sure your doctors are qualified to treat you? So often, in our communities, doctors are authority figures, and to our own detriment, we don't ask questions or push back for clarity.

Recently, a friend's brother went in for a prostate exam and colonoscopy. He's 45, a Black man in good health with no family history of cancer. He read that he should go in anyway. His doctor told him it was too early and that the tests would be done at age 50. The patient pushed back a bit. Wasn't it true that Black men should be tested earlier? The doctor, slightly annoyed, told him age 50 was fine if there was no family history.

The patient sought a second opinion. He was given both a prostate exam and a colonoscopy. The colonoscopy came back fine. His prostate exam showed that he had stage 1 prostate cancer.

That is harm. That is abuse. That initial doctor waving off his request for a screening is the kind of action we have to fight against. How do we do this? The best way you can be involved depends on what you're built for. Perhaps you can disseminate information about doctors to Black men in our communities. Perhaps you work in the medical community and you can spread information to doctors about how important it is to listen to their patients, especially Black men who don't get into the doctor's office as regularly as they need to anyway.

In 1932, the federal government funded a study on the long-term effects of untreated syphilis. They recruited 600 Black men, half of whom had syphilis, and made them think they were being treated for six months but actually left them untreated for *40 years*. Many of these men passed this disease to their partners. Many had children born with congenital versions of the disease. Just a few years into the experiment, penicillin was found to be a cure for syphilis. The subjects never received it. They were never even told it existed. *They weren't even told what disease they actually had.* The medical researchers told them they had "bad blood," a common colloquialism used in the community that encompasses many diseases. They obfuscated the disease, using that common term, knowing the subjects would question things more if the word "syphilis" was used.

What did the men receive in return? "Medical care" (although medical care begins with *first, do no harm,* and the medical staff were actively causing harm). The patients received money toward a funeral when they died. Nearly 100 would die directly from the disease.

Now, we live in a system where Black people can be dismissed by their health care providers when they ask questions and push for what they need. There is often a disconnect with the Hippocratic oath, *first, do no harm.* This system needs to be repaired. Health care and education should be a place where no one is harmed.

Of course, women have been similarly harmed by this government. Thousands of women were forcibly sterilized by doctors like J. Marion Sims, who until 2018 had a statue in Harlem dedicated to him as the father of modern gynecology.

In the nineteenth and twentieth centuries, Black women were sterilized by white supremacists who felt they could determine who was fit for parenthood. If a woman already had a child without being married or had any manner of mental health issues, it could be determined that she should be sterilized, sometimes without anesthesia. It was thought, among white folks, that Black people had thicker skin and had a higher threshold for pain.

In the 1840s, Sims brazenly conducted surgeries on many enslaved women. In the interest of the importance of saying names, let's note that the three names found in his research were Anarcha, Lucy and Betsey. Sims was developing a treatment for fistulas, but at the same time, he regularly brought in enslaved women for any number of surgeries including for fistulas, which prevented childbirth, making them less valuable to their owners.

From Sims's autobiography: "I made this proposition to the owners of the negroes: If you will give me Anarcha and Betsey for experiment, I agree to perform no experiment or operation on either of them to endanger their lives, and will not charge a cent for keeping them, but you must pay their taxes and clothe them."

When Sims began to treat white women, he used anesthesia.

That was in the nineteenth century, but today, it is noted that Black patients very often do not get the same amount of pain medication as white patients, and Black children receive less pain medication than white children when they have broken bones.

Let's not forget, the social services that many in our communities use and trust, like Medicaid, funded non-consensual sterilizations, and such sterilizations haven't stopped. California prisons sterilized hundreds of women as recently as 2010. Women that staffers expected to return to prison were sterilized on those grounds alone. The medical staff would make up an emergency reason for sterilization if women had multiple children, because they believed the women had too many children already.

This has happened in this country and around the world forever. It even had a nickname in the South: *a Mississippi appendectomy.*

Many states phased out these procedures in the 1970s. While abolitionists have fought to correct wrongs, very few states have done anything in the way of apologizing or setting up financial settlements.

We don't even realize we're walking by statues in honor of the things we've endured.

What You Know: You already know what it feels like to be harmed. Unfortunately, we all do. If we are to be abolitionists, if we are to champion the fight for humanity and decency, we must push for humanity and dignity within ourselves.

Let's go to something like schooling. For a while, the idea of increasing access to private schools, charter schools or lottery systems was (and in some places still is) being used to "improve" education. A lack of a decent education has historically been used to keep white supremacy in place.

Plucking out students to attend special schools, leaving behind those who don't have advocates, is *not* dismantling a racist educational system. It's only continuing the uneven process. It's literally harmful to leave students in an uneven school system with the rationale that some of the kids will do well elsewhere. In some states, the city will "take over" a school system if its test scores or other numbers don't fit expectations. When that happens, the parents and other leaders from the community have no input on what they actually need in order to have a system that works.

This is not just politics. This is not just education. This is harming young people.

There's a racist beginning to the creation of charter schools that people often pass over.

After *Brown v. Board of Education* was passed, many white cities and counties took things into their own hands to make sure their children would not attend integrated schools. In Prince Edward County, Virginia, they literally just shut down all public schools for five years to avoid having to integrate them. They used taxpayer dollars to establish white schools that were held in private buildings like churches. When the courts ordered that taxpayer dollars could not be used this way, white residents just put their kids in private schools.

The Black folks in the county didn't have options for

private schools. Many Black students were just out of school for several years. Just straight up, no education. Parents tried to gather their children as best they could and find family and community members who could tutor. But it was nothing like what even the segregated schools could offer.

At one point, when white citizens in the county were trying to get around trying to have Black students in their schools, other plans were discussed.

An attorney for Prince Edward County was quoted as saying, "Negroes could be let in and then chased out by setting high academic standards they could not maintain, by hazing if necessary, by economic pressures in some cases, etc. This should leave few Negroes in the white schools."

Unfortunately, many charter schools have similar policies that result in this kind of harm. Often, children with special needs, language delays, or bilingual needs are shut completely out of "choosing" schools that have higher scores and stats. And just as the white people in Prince Edward County sought to block Black students by making the academic requirements too rigorous, there are many cities where Black children aren't "good enough" to go to the very schools in their communities that their parents and loved ones support with tax dollars. Being left behind by a lack of educational support is harmful. We must fight it in every way we can.

As abolitionists, we know how important parenting is to everything we do to center our communities and make them whole. Every one of these 12 principles begins with the practice of being a whole and healthy person.

For example, there was a time when hospitals would give out infant formula bags before mothers were discharged. This is not a space to judge how mothers feed. Although we do have ample evidence that, if possible, breastfeeding can be beneficial, many women decide to formula feed because they are not supported with lactation nurses and other kinds of assistance. Breastfeeding is not easy, especially when a new mom is adjusting to so many other thoughts, feelings and needs.

How our medical community has handled this in the past has not been helpful. I have heard from women who say they were pushed to take home formula they didn't ask for. Some who were committed to breastfeeding even outright asked to not have the formula placed in their rooms, and it was done anyway, as a matter of hospital "policy." If these mothers had any difficulties breastfeeding, they were told to simply use formula.

On the other side, moms who were sure they knew right away that they would need to use formula either exclusively or as a supplement have been shamed in hospitals and given forms (as if that's something a mother should have to deal with after giving birth) explaining that breastfeeding is better.

Childbirth is a place where new mothers and parents as a whole should be supported and protected.

What can be done to stop this kind of harm? Progress is being made right now, in small but growing ways. In Minnesota, a program called Nurse-Family Partnership has been developed to help moms from childbirth until their child is age two. This is so much more than just *you'd better breastfeed* or *you'd better use formula*.

This is a concrete way that harm is healed and people in our community can have a start toward a life they deserve for themselves and their babies. A personal nurse comes to the home of first-time moms and gives counsel, support and help with diet for the baby and mom.

These are the programs we want to create and support. As well, moms who are in hospitals that don't have these programs need to know they will be treated with respect, too. We also want to make sure it's not a select few who have the support to even know about these programs.

Look around your community. As best as you can see, what needs to be done? Can you do it on your own? Probably not. Can you do it with the help of your abolitionist community? Absolutely, you can.

Whether it's the material on your airwaves, the food in your grocery stores, the medical care in your city, the transportation for workers or the school system for students—and beyond, you can make change. It's worth looking over it all to see how we stop harm from happening and stop the harm and abuse that already has.

Those Who Can Show: I briefly introduced Leah Lakshmi Piepzna-Samarasinha earlier. They are a multi-hyphenate individual: writer, organizer, performance artist, educator and cultural worker whose work is "about survivorhood, disability justice, transformative justice, queer femme of color lives, and Sri Lankan diaspora sitting in her room." Leah has been instrumental in my understanding of the intersection of ableism and racism as it relates to the prison and medical industrial complex.

Leah demonstrates that this care work is incredibly nuanced when it comes to breaking cycles of intimate and institutionalized violence, and there is a deep need to increase our capacity to hold the complexity of hurt. All of us have caused harm or have conspired with harm in some form—whether it was intentional or not—and so, just as much as we have the capacity to harm, we also have the capacity to transform. It is critical that when harm happens, we examine the root systems of harm in the life of the harm doer. This exploration enables us to see more clearly the whole human being and gives us a better sense of how we can approach them and support them in holding themselves accountable for the harm they have caused. (More on how we hold ourselves accountable in the next chapter.)

Harm reduction that is grounded in healing is more than just a theory or a practice, it is a life-affirming tradition that we have learned from our resilient ancestors who have survived brutal oppression and genocide. Leah's brilliance teaches us that our radical survival is dependent on our commitment to harm reduction. This shift in being in interdependence is a rigorous practice but a necessary one if we are to heal and make way for justice. This commitment to our mutual well-being is critical, because this is how we demonstrate that we see one another as valuable and not disposable and, most importantly, that we are worth fighting for.

How We'll Grow: How can you think about transformative justice? How can we repair harms for both those who are survivors and those who have been harmed? How do we curb the number of people who end up incarcerated for reporting their own harms? Why is it that young girls of color who have been abused are more likely to be processed as criminals than white girls, who more often are given referrals to health systems? How do we care for them? Transformative justice is about understanding cultural differences when working with people who have been harmed. It's about looking at people as individuals, not just numbers and stats and percentages. It's about allowing those harmed to have their own voices heard in the process of healing. So many times, if someone speaks out about being harmed, the procedural things that are supposed to be part of the process end up reharming instead of healing. Is there ever a space for someone to decide how much of the legal system they want to be involved with? Can anyone determine what is the best option for healing, not just for punishing? Restorative means just that, to gain justice by restoring someone. This process also helps to curb circular harm that sometimes is insidious in families and communities.

For example, in many communities, people who cause harm are not held accountable. People choose to not call law enforcement because they know that will cause more harm. Transformative justice is about ending the things that harm. It's about taking an abolitionist approach to ending child abuse, rape, domestic violence. We know these survivors need care and healing. What does that look like in a way that could transform them?

Transformative justice is a part of abolitionist practice that is both challenging and yet also effective— because we can work on it every day. (Remember your cauldron.)

In what instances can you see things through the lens of transformative justice? A teacher can choose to have a conversation with a student (a courageous conversation!) instead of shunting them to a dean or school cop. A parent can commit to therapy with a child labeled as "bad" or "troubled" before allowing any more labels to be applied—especially any that are tough to remove or will negatively impact the child in the future.

When we talk about transformative justice, just like when we talk about abolishing prisons, why is it that people immediately focus on what they think *can't* be done?

What if a serial killer who kills for fun is in our community, then what?

Yes, of course, communities must be protected from this harm (and these people need to be protected from themselves). But let's start with what we see and hear and live through *every single day* that can be managed with transformative justice and prison abolition.

We practice this principle so that we can interrupt harm for future generations. As a person with complex PTSD who has harmed and been harmed, I have a deep commitment to healing the harm caused but also preventing harm before it starts. When I think about the kind of world I want to raise my child in, I think about the ways I must teach him to be accountable, to not harm and to be present for his needs so he is able to track when he is being harmful. We practice and commit to not harming and abusing because we understand trauma actually stunts our ability to grow into fully evolved human beings. We understand that the world of racism and capitalism, patriarchy and ableism disrupts our ability to be fully connected to ourselves and others. Please take care to do this practice with your community of folks that you trust and are committed to.

The Real World: Do you scroll your timelines on social media, sneering at folks you call your friends? Do you screengrab posts and text them to friends, discussing someone's new hairstyle or new partner? Are you

petty? The definition of petty is something that's triv-
ial or of little importance. And that's why pettiness is
important for this chapter. When you think of not harming or abusing others, you usually think of large-scale
examples of harm: physical, emotional and otherwise.

But for some of us, even the ones who are committed to not harming or abusing others, social media is
where pettiness can rear its ugly head. If it's unchecked,
you can harm and abuse others without even realizing
it. You may write a nasty subtweet or post, or you might
engage in cyberbullying.

Social media is a recent phenomenon used largely
by millenials and Gen Z as a place to convey our
ideas and build careers. But, oftentimes, we use (me
included) our social media to harm and cancel each
other. Have you found yourself judging TikTok challenges with superiority or jealousy streaming through
you? This is an opportunity to recommit to our abolitionist practice.

One very simple way to commit to not harming and
abusing others: be mindful how you use social media.
Give yourself specific times to check in, not just scroll-
ing at bedtime for endless hours. Some people take
the apps off their phones and only use the browser versions of apps. Social media can be a space of creativity,
joy and connection. We also know that heavy use of social media can lead to depression, anxiety and loneli-
ness. Let's be mindful how we treat each other on and
offline.

GUIDING QUESTIONS

1. Have you been harmed or abused?
2. Were you able to engage in an accountability process for harm caused against you? If so, what did accountability look like?
3. Have you ever harmed or abused others?
4. Did you take accountability for harm caused? If so, what did accountability look like?

Practice Accountability

> Accountability does not have to be scary, though it will never be easy or comfortable. And it shouldn't be comfortable. True accountability, by its very nature, should push us to grow and change, to transform.
>
> —Mia Mingus, *Leaving Evidence*

Wait. What? Yes, we just said we would do our best to be intentional and not harm or abuse others.

But the likelihood is that at some point(s) you *will* cause harm. You'll have to deal with it. Honestly. Intentionally. In her blog, *Leaving Evidence*, Mia Mingus explains how to give a genuine apology and hold yourself accountable.

We all know those moments. We are tired, hungry, grumpy, any number of things can happen in our day-to-day lives that affect our behavior.

Sometimes, we just don't have an excuse.

I talked about being harsh with one of the members of my team. I left the meeting in tears and I didn't go back to the meeting. Over the next week or so, I asked other members of the team if they thought I should apologize. It was unanimous. My feelings were valid. My actions were not. I needed to take account-ability. I did.

As someone in a leadership position, even one that is very fluid, I have to be very clear on my mission, and I am very fortunate to have a team who can keep me in check. I don't need it often. I'm grateful to have it when I do.

When I was a child I was taught to apologize if I hurt someone physically or emotionally. It was usually an adult dictating what that actually meant, and I wasn't given practices or tools to be accountable for the harm I caused. There was often a lot of shame associated with behaving "badly," and so most of the time I would hide if I did anything that would have been perceived as "bad."

As an adult, I've learned that wronging someone is broader and more complex and nuanced than just do-ing something bad. Our actions are rarely that bad. We don't spend the day doing good and bad things. Plenty of our encounters fall somewhere on a spectrum.

The culture we live in teaches us to say "sorry" but also simultaneously teaches us that when we cause harm we are bad and unable to be redeemed or trans-formed. Whole groups of people in our culture deny harm caused just so they don't have to feel the self-shame that is associated with that harm they have par-ticipated in. We hear this from white folks and men and cis people. The moment that groups who hold privilege are asked to be accountable, there is a deep resistance to recognizing and then apologizing for that harm.

When we invest in accountability as a tool that moves us away from punishment, we get to feel the fullness and benefits of being accountable for what harm we have created. There are multiple times in my life where I have been accountable for the harmful conditions that were created in a dynamic. The moments when I have been accountable are the moments when I feel more present for connection.

It is a truly amazing moment when you hold yourself accountable and find the peace on the other side. Intention is always the way to bring forth clarity.

The times when I have not been accountable, I have felt a lingering discomfort that takes me away from myself and connection to others. Practicing accountability means we intentionally and actively apologize for the harm we caused, and we change our behavior so we don't cause that harm again. This kind of practice is articulated by abolitionists across our movement. It is critical for us to learn how to be accountable so we can transform the conditions of harm we've lived in.

If we want to see a world with all of the things we've discussed thus far, from courageous conversations to transformative justice, we must begin with our own accountability.

Different types of harm caused can lead to different ways of accountability. For example, we talked earlier about gossiping and backstabbing and backbiting, even (and perhaps especially) in jest. Do you need to approach the person you've spoken unkindly about? Not necessarily. Especially if they don't know. What you can do is commit to not getting pulled into that sort of harm. You don't have to speak highly of every person on Earth, of course. You don't have to make your mouth a weapon, either.

Are your conversations with your children brief? Do you get tense with your partner over small things? Are you tough on yourself?

When in conversation with someone, are you openly listening? Or are you just waiting for them to stop so you can speak?

Your work in abolition will require several layers of accountability. If you never find yourself in a position where you need to show accountability, you probably aren't making as much progress as you could be. It's like that old story about Formula 409, a cleaning agent. As the story goes, it was the 409th solution that they tried and finally got right, and they used the number for the name. You should just keep a running tally of getting it right, because it's all we can do: try not to cause harm and take accountability when we do.

How do you know when you're truly practicing accountability? Well, is it uncomfortable? Then you're probably doing it right. True accountability is not easy to do and takes effort. Expect to feel some discomfort.

Abolition is about righting injustices in a way that is sustainable. It's not giving someone the tools they need to exist in a racist system. It's doing away with the racist system. So in abolition, we are constantly looking for systems rooted in racism and patriarchy and dismantling them. We expect more than just a check and an apology for certain atrocities our people have dealt with.

You have to come up with more than just a *sorry* when you screw up.

Sometimes, you can apologize for something, and when asked what you're apologizing for, you might not even know exactly. (This is often true of young folks. They've been told *say sorry* so often that they've learned to just say it without actually taking accountability. They just want to not be in trouble and for the *thing* to be over, whatever it was.)

For some, seeing someone getting emotional is hard to take in. So we rush to apologize in the hopes that they will stop crying and return to "normal." We're taught to push back discomfort as quickly as possible. We try to apologize and hug to make it go away quickly.

But as abolitionists, sitting with discomfort is critical for taking accountability. Imagine that you have harmed someone. They confront you and tell you their thoughts. The most important thing you can do if you want to take accountability is just *listen*. So much discomfort and discord comes when people feel like they are not being heard. Often because someone wants to rush through the discomfort and skip to the apology.

Think about the next board meeting you'll have to

attend, the next critical meeting to discuss contaminated water in a community, the next meeting to discuss the defunding and demilitarization of the police. Do you want the people you're speaking about to just toss off a *Sorry*? Sorry that the water is contaminated. Sorry that incarcerated people are being sterilized without their consent. Sorry that we continue sending police into your communities with tanks and bombs. Now what? Are we done? Don't start crying please.

No, you want to be heard. Then, you want these agencies to be accountable for their actions. *Then*, together, actions can be taken.

That's what we expect in our work. So we should also expect it of ourselves.

Accountability means you'll be willingly and unfailingly honest about whatever your scenario is. Accountability means you won't procrastinate on righting the wrong or harm. Accountability means you must also explain how and why it won't happen again.

Instead of leaning in for a hug or to somehow comfort, listen. If that means there is anger, accept it. If that means there are tears, accept them. Sit with the discomfort of how this person feels. When it's time, you can ask, *are you okay?* Or, *is there more you need me to hear?* Be ready to hear them completely through. Sometimes, being present in that moment can look like you don't care or that you're being cold. Practice this. Practice doing things differently from how you may have been taught.

While someone may find it jarring that you're not swan diving into an apology but are instead standing up and being accountable, they will understand. They may very well do the same the next time they need to be accountable.

This principle is extremely necessary when it comes to things that have a crossover in our abolitionist work and in our own lives. There is built-in practice for accountability every moment in our day.

Don't confuse accountability with making amends. They are both worthy skills to have, but they are very different. Accountability comes first. It's actually the easiest of the two to begin to use. Accountability says, *I have harmed.* Full stop. Making amends comes later, sometimes immediately after, sometimes not. Amends is making a plan to undo or heal the harm done. First, you show up and hold yourself accountable, whether in person, via electronic correspondence (including social media, if that's how the harm was caused) or a handwritten letter. You let it be known that you are the person who has done the harm and explain that you're ready to take responsibility.

The reason why amends is separate is what amends looks like varies depending on the harm caused and what the person harmed needs to heal.

So many public figures show us how *not* to take accountability. Unfortunately, there are more examples of how it's done wrong than how it's done right. Let's learn from these.

Here's a whopper.

Actor Kevin Spacey, beloved in Hollywood for decades, had charges of sexual misconduct levied at him by one person. The number of accusers then quickly ballooned to nearly a dozen.

But when it came to being held accountable for the claims, Spacey did not just say, *this is not true, I did not do this.* His response was:

"If I did behave then as he describes, I owe him the sincerest apology for what would have been deeply inappropriate drunken behavior."

Where do we even begin with this non-accountability statement? First, if your apology, amends or statement of accountability has the word *if* in it, close your mouth and delete the document. Start over. There is no room for *if.* Because by definition, you're sowing seeds of doubt. *If I did behave . . .* is about as far away from accountability for harm as one can be.

The end of the statement is, *for what would have been deeply inappropriate drunken behavior.* This is the *why* of his behavior, which is completely unnecessary. If you cause harm, you need to explain that you did it. Period. The *why* is unnecessary and dilutes your accountability. The *why* is for you to sort, on your own or in therapy. The person you've harmed doesn't need to know why you did it and likely doesn't care if you haven't properly apologized.

The actual attempt at an apology is buried in Spacey's word soup: *I owe him the sincerest apology.*

Even then, he doesn't actually say it. He simply says he owes him an apology. Without actually giving him one.

A well-known reality star lost weight and then accepted compliments from those who said she stopped eating. When she was called out on how triggering and unhelpful that line of thinking could be, she tweeted out: "My intention is never to offend anyone, and I really apologize if I offended anyone."

Again, the word "if" is in there. She's not holding herself accountable for what she did. She's tossing off a nonapology for *anyone* she might have offended. It's as if she's still holding on to the idea that she didn't do anything wrong, but if you think otherwise . . .

Shrugs.

Interestingly enough, Kanye West, of all people, took proper accountability for his actions toward Taylor Swift when he took her moment at the 2009 VMAs to tell the audience that Beyoncé should have actually won the award.

He was persona non grata immediately, and on his blog, a few days later, he stated: "That was Taylor's big moment and I had no right to take it from her. I am truly sorry. I hope to apologize in person soon."

This is a perfect trifecta of accountability, apology and amends. He says plainly why it was wrong, what he did, that he apologizes and states what he wants to do next.

He ended up deleting it shortly after. Ten years later, well, he's still doing things that he needs to be held accountable for. He did show us, once upon a time, what accountability looks like.

So, when we think about accountability, think of it as "showing up," an expression we use often to mean we can let someone know we're committed to honoring whatever scenario it is.

Remember, you want to get accountability right, not just for the person you harmed—but for yourself. These situations don't disappear and you may end up continually offering accountability for harm you've caused in your past.

When a known Civil Rights leader was caught on a hot mic talking reckless about then-senator Barack Obama, his accountability was light.

"For any harm or hurt that this hot mic private conversation may have caused, I apologize." He later added, "I offer apologies because I don't want harm to come to this campaign."

He starts with the *why,* which is the first step to non-accountability. No one cares *why* it happened, only that it *did* happen. Then he makes it clear that he offers apologies so no harm would come to the campaign, not because it was just wrong.

There is zero accountability here. Particularly in movement work, there's no room for non-accountability gestures like this. We don't know what this Civil Rights leader and Obama's political relationship was before this. This kind of response is not a way to get to a point where amends can be made.

Congressman Joe Barton used this one as an apology: "If anything I have said this morning has been misconstrued to the opposite effect, I want to apologize for that misconstrued misconstruction."

Yeah, so much for accountability there.

Accountability is just that—an accounting of your abilities to handle your wrongs.

So, does anyone get it right? Well, Tiger Woods had this to say after his cheating scandal: "I was unfaithful. I had affairs. I cheated. What I did was not acceptable, and I am the only person to blame."

Lots of "I" statements. No *if*. He sets the accountability squarely on his own shoulders.

What to Read/Watch/See/Hear: Take a look at the eighth step in Alcoholics Anonymous. It states: "Made a list of all persons we had harmed, and became willing to make amends to them all."

Whether you're in recovery or not, it's an interesting concept to think about when it comes to accountability and healing harms. Keep in mind, those who are in this 12-step program traditionally work their way through all 12 steps and then immediately start back with the first step. Would you be willing to continually start over with a new accounting of those harmed? Yes, sounds frightening. But likely continually healing, as well.

What I Know: I know we're capable of this form of rigorous accountability. Abolitionist work will very often be about holding racists and those ensconced in patriarchy accountable for their harms. We are often pushing for recognition and repair, and it can be grueling. To know that we have to fight to get this from governments and corporations is to know how important it is to get these things from and for ourselves. Don't push it if you are not ready. I've said it before here and I'll say it again, we're human. We have to be gentle with ourselves and those we must push back against.

The most important (and difficult) aspect of accountability is being accountable to yourself. (Ack, I know.)

What does that look like?

It looks like intention. Do you want to wake up early each morning to do yoga? Work backward and see what steps are necessary to make that happen. What usually gets in the way? Do you stay up late binge-watching your favorite shows and then wake up late and miss your yoga class? Are you snacking heavy at night, which makes you not feel much like moving around in the morning? Are you over-extended in work or at home, which makes it easier to make plans than to execute them? Move back to the moment you make the intention, and think about what's happening at that moment that makes it difficult to have accountability for the things that harm yourself.

Writing down what your intentions are is a good step toward accountability. Erykah Badu once tweeted: "Write it down on real paper with a real pencil with real intent and watch it get real." It's true, the first step to accountability is holding yourself accountable at the very beginning. Write down what you want to see happen, how it will look throughout the process, and how you will keep yourself on target.

What I know is that this is serious work, it's not a simple task and it takes time and energy to practice and get it right. Or, to be more accurate, to get it near right.

What I know is that I still try daily to stay away from harming others. I know I consistently focus on how I can always be accountable if I do cause harm.

What You Know: Practicing accountability is not just about apologizing, it's about changing your actions and then repairing the harm that you caused. Take the United States and European nations, for example. They have never taken accountability for chattel slavery, not only for its impact on Black communities in the United States, but also across the globe. One way the U.S. can rectify the harm caused by chattel slavery is by honoring the demands for reparations. Reparations offer a real process for accountability. We can look at local reparations campaigns, like the one in Chicago. This campaign is led by Black organizations fighting for and alongside survivors of state violence to receive monetary reparations, a memorial, a torture survivor center and more. In Chicago, in the 1970s and 1980s, Commander Jon Burge tortured Black men in order to get them to agree to false allegations that were put on them by the Chicago police. This led to the incarceration of over one hundred Black men. After a hard-fought campaign, the Survivors of Torture by Jon Burge and the survivors' descendants were offered what they'd fought for. This is what being accountable looks like. Admit to harm caused, apologize for harm caused, seek to repair the harm and then implement the repair.

Those Who Can Show: Born in Korea and raised in the Caribbean, Mia Mingus uplifts her intersecting identities as a queer, physically disabled, transracial and transnational adoptee. These layers of experience have driven her commitment to liberation for all people, especially the most marginalized and overlooked— the disabled, survivors of sexual violence and those impacted by the prison system. Mia is a writer, educator and community organizer who has been involved in transformative justice work for more than 15 years and is one of the architects of the disability justice framework.

This framework is rooted in challenging the ableist supremacy that is so deeply pervasive in the United States and, arguably, the world. Disability justice is an intersectional, multi-issue framework that challenges the different forms of oppression and violence that disabled people experience.

Disability justice argues that ableism is often leveraged in service of white supremacy, patriarchy and male supremacy, transphobia, classism, and capitalism. Important components of disability justice are its exploration of interdependency, access and the practice of building alternatives that move us closer to a more just world for disabled people and their communities. Mia has challenged many of us in social justice movements that disability justice should not be an afterthought in the work that we do but should be a fundamental part of how we envision our freedom and liberation. Disabled people often experience mainstream social justice spaces as inaccessible spaces. For example, there may not be captions offered on educational videos, the places meetings are held may not have access ramps for people in wheelchairs, or there may be a lack of sign language interpreters in the room (to name a few).

It is important to acknowledge that this work of accessibility is not solely on the shoulders of those who need these services or resources, rather, what is at stake is the deliberate thought and effort to make access part of the infrastructure of how we effectively organize all of our people. It is exhausting for a disabled person to have to investigate whether they will feel welcome in our movement spaces—this information should be made readily available in all of our communications, all of our cultural content, events, etc.

We cannot simply stop at having elevators and interpreters, or other logistical matters—disability justice is also about what Mia calls the "immaterial things"— like the trauma of rejection and isolation that disabled people experience in an ableist world. Denying this aspect of accountability to our disabled kindred is also harmful. It is our collective responsibility to show up for all of our people and challenge all the ways in which we are complicit in ableism and must do better.

The impacts of the Covid-19 pandemic exposed

the many ways the current health care system and financial infrastructure in place do not, in fact, prioritize the welfare of people. For the first time, many abled people had to negotiate access and be confronted with the flagrant disregard for what disabled people had been needing and advocating for way before this public health crisis. Needs such as subsidized housing, better working conditions for workers, accessibility to online employment and education, etc. became the primary concern of the nation. Many institutions shifted quickly to respond to these needs—but only when able-bodied people demanded it. What will happen when there is a cure and things go "back to normal"?

There is an immense amount of harm this pandemic caused to disabled people, and able-bodied people must hold ourselves accountable to the ways in which we will continue to push for an infrastructure that honors disabled people's lives. There is exciting and creative work being done to establish sustainable mutual-aid models, where those of us with more privilege and resources can redistribute our wealth and create cross-class solidarity. This is an important step in practicing accountability, and there is more work to be done.

Mia continues to encourage us to practice accountability and create spaces of much compassion and grace as we reflect and pivot to a much more inclusive liberatory practice within our social justice movements. Mia proclaims that "practice yields the sharpest analysis," and while our movement spaces are not perfect, Mia reminds us that the goal is not perfection but a commitment to the real work of transformation. The work of accountability is complex, non-linear, and constantly shifting. There is a great fear and shame that is ingrained in movement spaces to always get it "right" in order to merit our credibility—but this allegiance to perfectionism misses the mark.

Transformational accountability requires that we take honest inventory of the harm we have caused, assess our commitment to transforming these behaviors, and be willing to actively and consistently build trust through vulnerability. Mia reminds us that healing and accountability must begin at the personal level because "[i]f we cannot handle the small things between us, how will we be able to handle the big things?" Mia's commitment to building the skills, relationships and structures that hold the complexities of transformative justice work is impeccable. Her frameworks offer us an opportunity to imagine, construct, and practice abolition at every moment.

We practice being accountable so we can disrupt the harmful conditions we have been raised in and learn new ways to be in relationship to each other. We practice accountability because it is something we are often not taught. We practice so we can have joyful and healed relationships. We practice accountability so we can break cycles of harm caused in our families and communities.

When my father was recovering from drug and

alcohol dependency, he went through the Alcoholics Anonymous 12-step program several times. One of the ways the program asks you to show up is through step eight: Make a list of all persons we have harmed, and become willing to make amends to them all.

While my father passed before he could get to step eight, I remember having many conversations with him where he identified being accountable and actively apologized for harm caused, as well as actively changed his behavior. As his daughter and someone in the community with him, his practice not only was inspiring but also taught me how I can be accountable to the people I love in my life.

Many people who are not in recovery still use this method of holding themselves accountable, both professionally and personally. It involves determining who you have harmed, getting honest about your role and then making a plan to absolve.

How We'll Grow: When it comes to keeping others accountable, insist on courageous conversations and listen closely to what they're saying and offering. You don't have to accept anyone's approach to accountability if it doesn't seem genuine or is flawed in any way. When someone harms, it's not up to the person who was harmed to figure it all out, make a judgment call and make a decision on if it's over or not. That happens when the person who has been harmed decides to let it go—if at all.

Accountability doesn't have a due date. There's no

time or space where you have to say your feelings have changed or you've made a particular decision about anything. Yes, this includes when you're being accountable to yourself.

Remember, this principle is not about giving or receiving apologies. This is about discerning culpability for harm in order to figure out what the next move is.

Keep track of your progress in this area. The more conscious you are of the large and small ways you work on this, the easier it is to practice.

I know of folks who do this sort of work together. Occasional meetings where accountability efforts are shared. You may have great tips on accountability at work with demanding jobs. Someone else might have particular skills with apologizing to parents, toddlers and teenagers.

Give and get your help wherever you can. We're all in this together.

The Real World: I've been in healing circles, ones where I have been called out and encouraged to be accountable for my actions. This does not feel good. Especially when the people surrounding you are ones that you know care for you, implicitly and explicitly, and only want the best for you. When you have to look into those eyes and see where you have fallen short, it makes you see things very clearly. You want to be a loved and trusted part of your community and you'll do whatever's necessary to heal your community. It is a very different feeling than depending on the state to determine your status. Most of us are much more likely to hold ourselves accountable *to* our community when it's coming directly *from* our community.

GUIDING QUESTIONS

1. Think of a time you have caused harm. What was the situation? Did you practice accountability?
2. How often do you apologize for harm you caused?
3. What is your reaction when someone asks you to be accountable for harm you caused?
4. Write out three things you plan on doing to be proactive in your accountability.

Embrace Non-Reformist Reform

> I would argue that abolition is the radical alternative. . . . The etymological meaning of radical is "root." So abolition allows us to get to the *root* of the problem. That is why it is the *radical* alternative. Abolition enables us to escape being trapped by the same framework, the same footprint, over and over again.
> —Angela Davis, Dream Defenders
> Sunday School 6/14

The idea of non-reformist reform is something that's hard for some to get on board with. Especially if you don't have a history in abolitionist work. To make it simple, non-reformist reform is the idea that we're not fighting to improve an existing, failed system. We are fighting for what we actually need within a brand-new system.

Here's an example: If you notice your lawn is dying out, reform would be sprinkling chemicals on it to feed the grass and kill the weeds. Non-reformist reform is upending the lawn and starting over with fresh sod and soil. Or let's say a school has disruptive students. Reform is using armed police officers as "school safety officers." Non-reformist reform is creating a school system where the staff and administration are leading the change and have what they need, without armed police officers inside.

As a young organizer, the first place I learned about abolition was the abolitionist group Critical Resistance. I was fortunate enough to go through one of their workshops where they detailed what it meant to be an abolitionist and why the current prison system was in fact an industry that we must abolish instead of reform. It was explained in that workshop that abolition was a vision for what is possible if we live in a world without police, prisons, courts, jails and surveillance.

A vision for what is possible. That phrase stuck with me. I liked the idea of having a vision for something. I felt like if I could shape my vision (and others) for abolition I could help shape my vision (and others) for literally anything. After my younger years of not being able to visualize anything beyond day-to-day survival, it felt freeing and promising to see things differently.

I learned in that workshop that we can actually work toward shrinking the police state. That I didn't have to compromise my beliefs in order to appease elected and appointed officials. I remember questioning the concept of reform. How could I be an abolitionist and also fight for reform? Critical resistance had an answer for that, as well. Non-reformist reform.

Reforms like body cameras don't get us closer to Black people's freedom, and they don't shrink the budget or power of the police and prison state. Our goal with non-reformist reforms is to shrink the police and prison state. We must be courageous and bold and demand a world with no jails and prisons.

We must demand our police departments and sheriff departments are defunded. Inside of those non-reformist reforms is a deep desire to build a world where Black people and all people get their needs met. A world without cages and handcuffs and police sirens. A non-reformist reform gets us close to abolition.

Body cameras are a good example of how so-called reform doesn't mean justice, transformative or otherwise. It seemed like a good idea, to some, once upon a time. The idea of wearable cameras has been around since the late 1990s, but it wasn't until the last decade that it's been done in large numbers. Right now, body cameras are used by nearly every major police department in the United States. So why has nothing changed? Why are unarmed Black men and women still being shot dead in the street?

The officer who killed George Floyd was wearing a body camera. So why is it that the true story was captured by bystanders and not from his body cam? Despite the fact that a body camera was useless in this case, some organizers and government officials are pushing to deploy more and more body cameras to appease our demands for police accountability. There is no data that proves that body cameras make communities safer, but cities continue to invest more and more community dollars that could be used to hire actual support for their over-policed residents.

Republicans, not known to support non-reformist reform (or reform at all), have been known to support an increase in the use of body cameras. In some states, adopting the use of body cameras by police officers is a way to build up trust with their constituents. But if the officers are not properly equipped to respect and protect their communities, as many of them are not, body cameras are just window dressing. It's a bandage on an open wound.

Obama said it this way back in 2015: "It's not a panacea. It has to be embedded in a broader change in culture and a legal framework that ensures that people's privacy is respected."

Herein lies just part of the problem. There's no unified way that cities handle when and how officers turn their cameras on and off. There is no unified way that these recordings are stored and shared with the public. Depending on where you live and what the laws are, you could never see the footage.

Some police departments allow officers to edit footage before it is shared. What exactly is the point of cops having body cams if we can't trust what we're seeing?

Because of where I live and what I've seen and how long I've been in the world of activism, I've always had a healthy understanding that body cameras have never been the answer.

I know that if I file a complaint of misconduct

against a police officer and I know the officer's body cam was on, I have no right to see the footage or use it in court. So how is that helpful? How is this making police officers more accountable?

Why is it that in New York City, the Civilian Complaint Review Board has reported that, many times, they have asked for body cam footage in cases—and received nothing? Sometimes they are told that the footage has been lost—only for it to be leaked to the media later.

When it's likely that these body cams show police officers in wrongdoing, that footage is almost never released to help a case proceed.

Why would communities expect wearable tech to change police behavior? It doesn't. A few small studies showed officers who wear cameras are less likely to have complaints from the community. But a study done with thousands of officers showed an insignificant difference.

It's human behavior that if you're wearing a camera all the time, at some point you'll continue whatever behaviors you've always had. Which is why we're still seeing officers doing things like planting drugs on innocent people, right in view of the body camera that's recording. And why are officers often allowed to turn the cameras on and off at will?

To put this in perspective, the cameras face outward for officers to record what they're seeing. It's not the same as keeping officers accountable. It's not telling us what *we* see. And we still are not getting access to this information—so what's the point?

It's not as if this idea of body cams worn by officers has been connected to a decrease in police brutality.

Police departments need to be abolished and defunded. Period. We know how to think bigger than body cams and review boards. We can take care of our communities differently—and still effectively. We can actually rehabilitate instead of punish.

It goes beyond policing. Reforms ultimately keep the greater society the same, with some minor approaches to change. They actually maintain, support and increase the status quo and don't approach the root causes.

André Gorz, who coined the term "non-reformist reform," had a very simple framework for action. He believed in creating communities and societies that were based on human needs, not on economic systems.

It may be hard for some to understand that non-reformist reform is absolutely doable. Not only is it doable, it's crucial.

This principle is important. Because this is where we begin to understand how capitalism has prioritized profit over people. This system has not served us and needs to change in order for it to do so. Here's an example: Instead of a society where car manufacturing and marketing is prominent, to the point where every American household needs to own (by finance) two vehicles, what if our infrastructure and transportation systems decreased the number of people who needed cars and increased the number who could instead rely on a well-tuned and inexpensive public transportation system? This would be transforming several systems at once, when you include the win of having less pollution when we have fewer cars on the road.

What also must be understood is that non-reformist reform does not come from the top down, economically. This is not a theory where you assume the high-end capitalist society will support change. Also, the people most in need of change are completely capable of changing these systems themselves. This is not a situation where a certain group sits in a conference room or a lecture hall and works out how to enact non-reformist reform. The people on the ground can build this system. According to Gorz: "The people are active in reordering social relationships, diagnosing social inequalities, and mobilizing for a better way of socially organizing the world."

A common example of non-reformist reform is the idea of strikes. For hundreds of years, workers going on strike to gain things like higher pay or safety measures has been a mainstay. Over the years, organizers have helped strikers with their demands and seeing them through. But ultimately, strikes only keep capitalist ownership in power. A strike is coming, they know what to do, they meet the demands—or not—and life goes on. But if the employees demand control of what happens on a day-to-day basis, it's a different world and more sustainable model. In that case, empowered workers have an ongoing initiative to constantly improve the workplace, instead of simply waiting for when a strike is needed. This is stirring the cauldron—instead of just letting it boil over and cleaning it up, repeatedly.

Sometimes, the idea of non-reformist reform is difficult to put in place because it's believed that the current system is working. An example is the Red Cross and NGOs, which work in places like Haiti. After the 2010 earthquake, $1.4 billion was donated to Haiti from Americans alone. Even two years after the earthquake, however, many Haitians were still living in substandard housing with little access to clean drinking water.

After the celebrities and politicians left the country, the people of Haiti were out of the media spotlight. The money was still flowing through, but it was still not changing their quality of life.

The fact is that most organizations were best at day-one planning. They were giving out tarps in the days, weeks, and months after the earthquake but not working toward better, permanent housing, using the people's ideas as a gauge of what could and should be done—and how. Non-reformist reforms are about structural change rather than putting a Band-aid on the wound. We have to uproot systems and build something new.

What to Read/Watch/See/Hear: *Locking Up Our Own: Crime and Punishment in Black America* by James Forman Jr. is a stunning and necessary look at how much Black people have contributed to mass incarceration. The "good" politicians who were supposed to have our best interests in mind. The warped way that previous generations failed our younger people. The author, a public defender, once looked around a courtroom while he was defending a 15-year-old and noticed that every single person who would be involved in the process of locking this young man up—from the judge to the jury to the prosecutor to the bailiffs—was Black. They all spent every day locking up Black people. He quotes Jesse Jackson, who once said, "No one has the right to kill our children. I won't take it from the Klan with a rope; I won't take it from a neighbor with dope."

The neighbor with the dope is on the same level with a Klansman? Jackson believed that the people in our community, selling drugs that were purposely dropped into our communities, were the enemy? Abolition becomes a North Star for our political values and practices. We can't equate a drug dealer with a Klansman, and we can't use punishment as a way to deal with poverty.

What I Know: For over a decade the LA No More Jails campaign (now known as Justice LA) has organized against the $3.5 billion jail construction plan looming over the Los Angeles community. For more than a decade, the Los Angeles–based coalition worked alongside over 15 organizations to push the Los Angeles County Board of Supervisors and the Los Angeles Sheriff's Department to stop wasting billions of dollars on incarceration and criminalization and instead real-locate those dollars toward community resources.

For more than ten years LA No More Jails was essentially laughed at, and we were told our vision for Los Angeles was naive and uninformed. After every single meeting we had with an elected official who told us we would not be able to win over the community with the No More Jails message, we organized harder. We never relinquished our vision of abolition, and in fact we continued to organize ourselves toward non-reformist reforms.

We knew that the only way to fight against jail expansion was to keep organizing, keep getting stronger, and leverage every opportunity to remind the local government that the fight against mass criminalization is a fight we would continue until they officially stopped jail expansion in Los Angeles. By the time 2016 rolled around, we were being told that the building of the new women's jail, the closure of the men's central jail and the rebuilding of a mental health jail were official and there was no more room to fight against the jail plans.

Many of us saw an opportunity with the election of Trump and the election of a new county board of supervisors. These supervisors had inherited the jail plans and they could, in theory, not only reverse the plans but chart a new way forward.

In 2017, a group of us rebranded LA No More Jails as Justice Los Angeles. We wanted to develop a broad-tent coalition not only across Los Angeles but also across the country. There were multiple counties fighting against jail expansion. We saw ourselves situated as part of a national fight against the criminalization of our communities. Justice LA launched in the summer of 2017, led by powerful young leaders directly impacted by the carceral system. The launch was multi-pronged.

We used art—100 replica jail beds placed in the middle of Downtown Los Angeles in front of the county board of supervisors building. We used public testimony—300 people went into the board meeting while many of us protested outside its doors; and we used mass engagement—we brought some of the best thinkers and cultural workers together to launch the Justice LA campaign. We knew this launch had to not just feel big but also be big. We needed the county to understand that after ten years of fighting us, they needed to move forward with what the community was demanding.

Our combination of direct visual art, words from the community and hundreds of citizens inside the meeting and more outside felt like a ten-year effort—because it was.

Dignity and Power Now, Youth Justice Coalition, La Defensa, CURB and Frontline Wellness Network have become the central organizations that led the Justice LA Coalition to victory.

Joining forces with like-minded groups is the best way to push for a large issue. You can band together for funds, staffing, planning and incidentals. It's super difficult for any one org to handle an event like that one, and I remember being very grateful that we had the support we did and we got the outcome we worked hard for.

What You Know: Cash bail is a complete failure in most cities, and you should look up what's happening in your city/state. Some governments have started to change the system, but there are many more places where it needs to be abolished.

In most cities, if someone is represented by a private lawyer, they will see a judge within 24 hours and then some sort of conditional release will be arranged. Most cities have many options for this release but lean on the one that brings in the most money: cash bail. If you don't have the cash (and the average bail is $55,000, more than the average American citizen makes in a year), you sit in jail until your court date or plea bargain. Or, if you have the option, you can hopefully have someone put up collateral to guarantee your appearance in court. Almost always, there's a bondsman in the mix, and their office will get 10 percent of the bail amount; whether the person is later found innocent doesn't matter. It's a billion-dollar industry made of amounts almost exclusively drawn from low-income communities. We have become a nation of people who expect to have to pay to be free.

We are also a nation of people who have stories like that of Kalief Browder, a 16-year-old from the Bronx who had a dizzying and ultimately fatal experience with pretrial intervention. He did not qualify for bail after an alleged theft of a backpack because he had a parole violation, which automatically makes it impossible to have a bail set, even when you're 16 years old and the (alleged) offense is a stolen backpack. He sat in jail awaiting trial for three years.

Three *years*.

The prison and pretrial intervention system failed Kalief for three years and created a broken vessel of a young man who still found a way to write about the prison system after he was released.

(He was finally released after three years only because the witness to the backpack theft left the country and the state had no other evidence but this eyewitness testimony, which had proven to be shaky, at best. Two years later, Kalief hanged himself.)

When we read up on Kalief's story and the stories of others who have been exploited in this way by an unjust system, we see that not just something must change, everything must change.

While there are celebrities who will take a meeting with a politician to see a single person freed—with the best of intentions—that is not abolition. That's reform, not non-reformist reform. Non-reformist reform is about seeing prisons shut down, seeing cages and handcuffs done away with. Seeing a world where people are not solely punished but healed.

Those Who Can Show: Ruth Gilmore tells a story about an event where she was the keynote speaker. There was a group of middle school kids from the town who heard she was a "prison abolitionist." They asked someone at the conference if she could come and speak with them. They wanted to know what a prison abolitionist was. She told them, plain and simple: don't build any new prisons, start closing the existing prisons and have a plan in place to support these communities without cages and bars.

For a moment, she thought they might cheer her on. Perhaps they had been affected by the prison system and would support her idealism.

Except not. They were *pissed*. Why close the jails? Where would the criminals go? Where would the murderers go? What about people who have guns who are not supposed to? Getting rid of jails doesn't get rid of the bad people.

This is true, she said. Does putting them in jail make the so-called bad people good?

Gilmore explains that for the next half hour or so, she slowly and methodically explained abolitionist practice to these 12-year-olds. They listened. (And they side-eyed.) She said that speaking to that audience showed her the audacity of her beliefs. We are often so hewn to what we know that switching to non-reformist reform can feel impossible. But it's not. Read. Write. Grow. At the end of the event, the students reported to the adults what they'd learned from the speakers. They had come around to one thing that surprised them all: prisons needed to be abolished.

How We'll Grow: This is a big step. If having a

courageous conversation is something that takes effort, tackling non-reformist reform is many times that. It may go against your upbringing or just what you've studied and what you've believed. What we need to grow here is imagination. This is where sitting across from other people (in person or on Zoom, alas) and just getting into the nuts and bolts of non-reformist reform becomes important. Read the major pieces on the topic, write out questions and then ask them. Figure out what organizations, both nationally and on the local level, are in line with what you're thinking. Map out your own personal strategy. It could be as simple as explaining to others what you've recently learned. Did you read a book on abolitionist practice that was helpful? Pass it along. Slip in a note and bookmark the passages that meant something to you. Make yourself available to discuss. We inch along and we sprint, too.

The Real World: The visual display we used for the prison abolition project brings up something that's very important: art as abolition. It's always been a part of the process for me to merge those parts of my life. My art deeply informs my role as an abolitionist, and my abolitionist work is clearly a main theme in my art. Art is an extension of my political values. Often as I am developing my art, I sit in silence, allowing for imagination to help me get clarity on how I want to aestheticize my abolitionist work. It can be soothing, motivating and inspiring.

GUIDING QUESTIONS

1. Name a societal ill that doesn't seem to have a solution. What feels impossible about resolving this societal ill?
2. What is an example of how non-reformist reform works?
3. Is there a non-reformist reform scenario that would be difficult for you to put in place?

Build Community

Without community, there is no liberation.
—Audre Lorde

So much of the work of abolition is building a container in which to practice abolitionist culture. The way to build that culture is to build a team. To build a community. This isn't necessarily based on geography or even on proximity. There are abolitionist teams who work internationally who never meet face-to-face.

This is especially true now, when we live in a whole new world and people are still working from home and finding interesting backgrounds on Zoom. We're not always in person together, but it doesn't mean we can't mobilize and organize successfully.

The concept of community building is really about whom we can trust, whom we can feel emotionally, spiritually and physically safe with, as well as reciprocal accountability. These are the key factors when building the community you want to be evolving inside of. How we practice abolition is critical.

For the last 20 years I have been a part of an intentional abolitionist community. We are multi-racial, inter-faith, multi-gender, multi-class, differently abled, pro-Black, pro-trans, pro-queer, pro-poly and we deeply believe in the theory and practice of abolition. In different iterations, our community has lived communally, met weekly for our social event, called "Tribes Day," and held monthly retreats to talk courageously about how we impact each other and the ways we can grow individually and collectively.

We have worked really hard to make sure everyone feels seen and heard in our community. We want to grow—as individuals and as a collective—so it's important that we check in on each other as often as we can to stay centered on the ideals we believe in.

As we have grown older, we've dealt with loss, gentrification and tending to our own familial needs. We don't all live in the same neighborhood, region or country, but we still consider one another a community.

Yes, community can be anywhere you need it to be.

You need every principle we've discussed thus far in order to make this one work. This work can't be done alone. Can you start alone? Yes. Can you read alone and think alone and marinate on teachings alone? Absolutely. No matter what level your work will take you to, it will likely require you to join or build a community—whether it's a weekly meeting at your kitchen table or a Zoom lecture with hundreds.

How do you build a community? What does it look like to you?

I know that my scenario, an intentional and purposeful work-life community with like-minded comrades, puts me in a very privileged position. I am very aware of that. So I can only say: it is attainable. It takes work, but it is attainable.

Perhaps your community begins with just yourself. You add one more person. This is a community! Don't think for a moment that if it's less than a dozen people, it's not a community. You start where you are, strengthen the bonds as tight as you can and then add on as it makes sense to do so. Community building is fluid and ever changing. Start with how you plan to communicate. Will you try to meet in person? What are your schedules, and how much time per week can you give to building community? Compare work and life schedules and see what makes sense. Offer fine details that help a community grow stronger through future plans, potential job or home changes. What do you want from this work? How often should you take a step back and evaluate your past, present and future?

What needs to happen as your community grows? You'll need to make sure there are clearly defined roles and everyone knows what's expected of them. Even if it causes slight conflict at the beginning, it's more important to have that discomfort now than when you have a community of 50 people who are all resentful because no one has clearly defined roles.

The community for this work doesn't need to mirror everyone's role in the outside world. If Ellen is an attorney who specializes in immigration law and she wants to work on that in the community—of course, that's what she should do. If Ellen is an attorney who specializes in immigration law but she actually wants to make the coffee for every meeting, clean up afterward and oversee the children's area, then that must be okay.

A community's development must be led from within. People should be able to define themselves not by their labels but by what suits them. Of course, if you have a member who speaks Spanish or French or Haitian Creole, it would be hoped that they would help as needed. But if someone's full-time job is translating and that part of their brain is simply exhausted, it might make sense to hire a translator as needed. Just because someone *can* do something doesn't mean they are the best person for that task. Consent is a critical practice.

Figuring out who does what may be the more challenging part of setting up a growing community. Everyone should have a role to play, so that there's an equal feeling of belonging. Figuring out what those roles should look like is not always (or ever) simple to do.

We've already talked about how to interact with one another; this is when it gets real. You're not fond of someone's ideas, and they can tell. You both choke up and don't speak at meetings—and the frostiness can be felt throughout the room. You're not ready to have a courageous conversation. You might just need some space. One of you can take a break from the regular meeting until you have some time to process the feelings and move on from them.

A strong community has plans for relationships that occur within it. Like-minded people, especially when dealing with something as intense as abolition, are likely to grow close to one another, and that can manifest in many ways, from besties to friends with benefits to poly long-term relationships. It can all strengthen the community. Or it can explode it to bits.

Will your community have a hands-off rule in place, with no in-house sexual relationships between members? How will you enforce that? What will happen to those who flout the rule? Or will there be a do-as-you-please-we're-all-grown mentality? What are the risks there and how will you deal with the consequences?

What should your meetings and get-togethers be like? In Alcoholics Anonymous, each organized meeting has several options. It can be an open meeting, which means anyone can attend, whether or not they are alcoholics, including students and teachers and anyone doing research. It can be a closed meeting, where everyone must identify as having a problem with alcohol and is expected to share their first name with the group for accountability. With some groups, you can't attend your first meeting unless you've been sober for 24 hours; with others, you can come straight from the bar. There are gender-specific meetings; LGBTQIA+-only meetings; Big Book meetings, where they mostly read AA literature; and step meetings, where they discuss one of the 12 steps and start at the first step every 12 weeks.

The list of possibilities goes on and on with different types of meetings that all work under the AA umbrella and have the same common goal. Keep that in mind as you build your community. It should be set up to work for what you're building. There's no need to make it identical to anything else you know. As long as you all can communicate, deal with conflict and reflect on your progress, your community will grow.

Bring that imagination principle to community building. Think about what you want to see and achieve, not just what you have seen in the past. Imagine. Build your capacity to see your community beyond what it has traditionally been perceived as.

Over the years, communities have been decimated by infighting. In some cases, external forces infiltrated communities to sow discord and keep them from becoming too powerful. If your community has any form of power, expect that you are known and that you may one day be worthy of infiltration.

Leadership is important. Will there be a single leader and co-leaders or deputies? Will people be appointed or elected? Will there be term limits? Can people be suspended? Ejected? On the basis of what? Because you may be building your community from scratch, leadership is something you may need to handle by default. Then, at some point, be ready to reevaluate what works and where your skill set is best used.

Doing movement work doesn't mean it has to be all doom and gloom and statistics and court cases. How will your community unwind and team build? How will you make sure you are not overwhelmed and overworked? Good community work doesn't come with exhausted or worn-down community members. Is there a monthly movie night? (Most streaming services offer a way to watch films "together" at a specific time.) Is there a recipe night where people bring their favorite dish or takeout from a favorite restaurant? Food brings people together. So do massages and mani-pedis.

As your community grows and solidifies, your own thoughts toward the ideals of the community will change. It could happen as your community gains greater wins or deals with greater challenges. It could happen as members' thoughts change on your stated ideals. It could happen as the average age of your community members becomes younger. Either way, things will change and you need to be prepared for that.

Being nimble is also important. Whatever your community needs, both internally and in the greater world, try to stay educated on the issues that are important. It's tough to do. Elections are happening consistently, bills are constantly being introduced and reintroduced in Congress, and op-eds that push opinion on different topics, news specials, documentaries, funded studies and research are always fighting for attention—there's a lot going on that will affect abolitionists, and staying on top of it all will be a central theme in community building. Creating an infrastructure where community members can take on different aspects of this work is key to establishing a sustainable community.

What to Read/Watch/See/Hear: The National Museum of African American History and Culture has a series of lesson plans on Black community building that can be used in or out of a formal education setting. If you are already on your way to building your team, a good resource to check out is a workbook by Mariame Kaba and Shira Hassan called *Fumbling Towards Repair.* This workbook is a valuable resource that can provide best practices in addressing interpersonal harm and violence in communities.

What I Know: As the mother of a son who asks questions and is beginning to ask how the world works, I know how important it is to fill up our children's minds as early and as quickly as we can. They are sponges, and sitting down with them, cutting through all of the daily noise of all of our lives, is the best thing we can offer them. When your child starts playing make-believe, pretending to eat food, take orders and tuck in animals, that's when you know that imagination is ramping up and they are ready to make sense of their world.

For me, part of my story is that while my home life wasn't able to always provide that kind of imaginative support, at some point I started seeking it out myself. If I hadn't gotten randomly sent to audition for a rigorous performing arts school in junior high—I don't know where I'd be. Because my mom wasn't focused on that. Once I saw that imagination, felt it, tasted it, that was it. I never let go. I knew it was there. I just didn't know what it was—or what to do with it.

We can't underestimate the importance of elders in our community. They can be the backbone of a community (not by default). Those who choose to build are invaluable. I was blessed to have a relationship with my great-grandmother throughout my childhood. She passed when I was twenty-one. Every time I told her I wanted to have an impromptu show for her, she would roll her eyes but she was there. She gave me 100 percent of her attention. Let's practice being fully present with each other. Presence is invaluable.

What You Know: Community building can seem daunting, but most of us are wired to do it. Our family of origin is often our first community. We may not build it from the ground up, but it's our first understanding of what community building looks like, for better or for worse. You'll have some moments where you're not sure if what you're building is sustainable. As long as you're giving it thought, each step will help you sort your goals.

You also know that we have to focus on self in order to build a community. If for any reason you are not in the best space personally, any community you try to build will not have a solid foundation. Before you begin a community, think, what are your own goals, personal and professional? What are you doing to make them happen? Are you stunted in any way? What about your health? Are there any health screenings or doctor/dentist appointments that you're overdue for?

Don't let community building become something else to divert you from the important things. There's no sense in building organizations and communities to talk about bettering our world when you're overdue for a mammogram or a prostate screening. Get a clean bill of health. Maybe you get your finances together before you start organizing. You can get a free credit report and see where you stand and what you want your next personal goal to be.

Mind, body and soul should be calibrated before you take over the world.

Those Who Can Show: Kendrick Sampson was born and raised in the suburbs of Houston, Texas, the son of Daphne Smith Sampson and Hoyle Sampson Sr. Growing up biracial, he reflects that while his lighter complexion afforded him certain privileges, he also experienced an internalized self-hatred for not "being enough" of one thing or the other; he now recognizes this is really the colorism we all learn from white supremacist culture.

As a teenager, Sampson's experiences with systemic injustice intensified—he remembers being pulled out of his car at gunpoint by a police officer who accused him of stealing his mother's car. The officer claimed that Kendrick "fit the description," but after discrediting the baseless accusations, the young Kendrick was left disturbed and uneasy.

It became clear to him that, no matter how "light skinned" he appears, he is still a Black man in the eyes of law enforcement. This interaction would later be foundational in his development as an abolitionist freedom fighter and would greatly shape the trajectory of his acting career in Los Angeles, California. In just a few short years, Kendrick has successfully built a powerful and radical community of people at every level of the entertainment industry that is challenging the industry to be an ally in amplifying the voices, stories and vision of a world that is just for everyone.

In 2019, Kendrick founded BLD PWR, a nonprofit initiative. His organization is successfully connecting people in his hometown in Texas to the work that is happening in Los Angeles and across the nation— binding together a multitude of experiences, analyses and wisdoms that are enriching our movement for the better.

Kendrick is a master community builder and communicator—he has successfully built bridges in spaces that would intimidate most, but he has done it unapologetically and confronted age-old institutions with searing, acute criticism. He is unabashed in his interviews, candidly stating that "[Hollywood is] actually an oppressive capitalist, white supremacist system" that has been complicit in perpetuating the culture of violence in Black and Brown communities in the United States and in the world. Kendrick calls out this billion-dollar industry for the harmful systems it has created internally within its privileged walls and the oppressive culture it has shaped through narratives that reinforce police violence and anti-Blackness in television and film. Kendrick is relentless and refuses to believe that this creative and imaginative industry cannot do better. Through the organizing efficacy of BLD PWR, he is transforming the way that mainstream media is representing the uprisings that center the defunding of police in defense of Black lives. Taking it a step further, Kendrick co-wrote a letter that was signed by more than 300 Black actors that urges the entertainment industry at large to divest from police and invest in the Black community. The letter bluntly states that "[t]he lack of a true commitment to inclusion and institutional support has only reinforced Hollywood's legacy of white supremacy. This is not only in storytelling. It is cultural and systemic in Hollywood."

The basis of his key ideas is that donations, while important to fund these movements, are not enough and, for Kendrick, are only superficial and do not translate to the structural transformation that needs to take place if Black lives are to be truly valued.

If you follow Kendrick on his social media platforms, you can catch a glimpse of his astute tactics—he reels you in with Hollywood allure (read: a headshot or shirtless selfie) and, once he clickbaits you, you read the fine print and you realize that he's actually educating you on the latest action or campaign that you should be supporting. His ability to leverage his unique position as a storyteller to deepen, complicate and expand our narratives has been vital in this movement to transform how we are represented. A cultural shift in mainstream media is key if we are to win, because the most difficult part of fighting for our freedom is being able to imagine what our freedom can look like and then fighting like hell to make it a reality. Kendrick is training and leading the vanguard of creatives who will authentically tell our stories and open up the pathways where abolition, healing, and freedom are on the screen and in daily lived practices.

How We'll Grow: Plain and simple: without community, we don't get free. Even though many communities, like the Black Panthers and the Nation of Islam, were flawed, both in their beginnings and at their heights, we can learn from them and avoid the bumps we know will be in the road waiting for us.

Think long-term. What happens if you pivot in a different direction, can your built community stand on its own? Can you step away from a community you've built? Absolutely! It's a testament to the strength of what you've built when you can move on and know that the ideals you've put into place are there. Nimble is good. Audre Lorde's life, spent building communities, is an example of how it looks when it's time to move on and set up a new (or just an additional) community. Every group will not fill every person's needs, creatively or otherwise. You can't expect every community to be a perfect reflection of yourself. It wouldn't work well if it was. Our communities can benefit from creating a space for nuance and complexity. This is how we learn and grow together.

The Real World: In the early days of BLM, we received a large donation from a (very) famous celebrity. We were very appreciative and knew exactly how the money would be best spent. We were also nervous. The celebrity was very firm—keep it anonymous. In the early days of our social justice era, people in certain industries wanted to keep their involvement with Black Lives Matter quiet. (I'm happy to see that people are much more transparent now about these things.) We gave our word that we would keep it to ourselves. Then, another comrade in the movement spilled the beans on social media. They were exhausted from hearing disparaging comments being made about this person. So they posted: Celeb XYZ just donated to BLM so *there*. Oof. Even though the comrade wasn't an officer within BLM, they were a reliable source, and the press started to swarm me and my co-founders to find out if it was true. Obviously, we couldn't lie.

Here's where your community comes in. For me, let's call my main support during this time Benny. He called the day our benefactor's identity was revealed. I was shaking with nerves. Personally and professionally, I wasn't prepared for this kind of scandal. I had given this person my word! It wasn't my fault, but no one wants to hear that.

Benny called me every hour on the hour, offering

advice, giving me only necessary updates and guidance. He made sure I ate, took breaths, remembered that this, too, would pass. In that particular moment, when the other members of my different communities were laden with their own issues and weren't able to show up for me, Benny did.

He reminded me that it was a luxury problem. Someone had given us our largest donation to date. It was going to help a lot of people, I had done the best I could to keep it quiet and it just didn't work out that way. When I'm in the real world, just a human putting one foot in front of the other, I need the Bennys in my life to show up for me unexpectedly. My community sometimes has community within it, and that's very precious to me. You will have that moment. Make sure you are nurturing the relationships with the Bennys in your life and community.

GUIDING QUESTIONS

1. Do you belong to an established community of any sort?
2. Do they have goals as a group?
3. Do you have an idea of what your ideal community looks like? Describe it.
4. Are you familiar with historical, established communities and how they were able to maintain? Or not maintain?

Value Interpersonal Relationships

We do this because the world we live in is a house on fire and the people we love are burning.
—Sandra Cisneros

We are taught that our friendships are not our most valuable relationships or worth fighting for. Especially when someone has hurt us. We are often taught that people are disposable and are unable to transform and heal. These messages are all throughout the media. Whether it's every reality show that ends with "friends" physically abusing each other or lying about one another to other "friends" or it's a social media beef that ends up in people blocking and then "canceling" each other because they don't trust each other any longer.

Cancel culture in general doesn't value interpersonal relationships. Cancel culture is like fast food and fast fashion. We're making snap decisions. We wouldn't cancel our parents, children, loved ones or friends this way. When we have conflict, we don't imagine simply walking away. Cancel culture is more often used in scenarios where the person or product wasn't going to be essential to our day-to-day lives anyway. Why are we canceling celebrities who don't have an effect on our bottom line? Why are we canceling fashion lines that don't align with our anti-capitalist views anyway?

The cancel culture in reality television is supposed to be entertaining. While it can pull you in, it doesn't quite entertain as much as it fascinates. What we model on television also gets modeled in the actual real world. It's not possible to absorb that kind of culture and not re-recreate it. That won't work if we want to value interpersonal relationships.

Interpersonal relationships are important because they are how we build our communities, and healthy connections to other human beings help build strong societies. The role of an abolitionist is to recognize the inherent value of human life and human connection. It is why we believe everyone has the capacity to transform, heal and be accountable for harm caused.

People are creating their own families more and more. Particularly when our families of origin are not healthy. Or are outright toxic and harmful to us.

It's a well-worn expression: you can't choose your family. But we know that we *can* create families by valuing interpersonal relationships.

The first step is to not base your relationships on labels we've been given in the past. You may have a family-of-origin sister whom you love. But your room-mate is who you're closest to and would call in case of an emergency.

A friend and I discussed this, and she told me about her interpersonal relationships and how they're valued. She doesn't explain her family to people because she's often not believed or people have dismissive and judg-mental things to say about how it can't work.

My friend was married for a decade. We'll call her Pam. Her wife Sarah brought a young daughter to the relationship, and Pam and Sarah later had one daughter together. Pam has never referred to her older daughter as a step. She has two daughters, period. Sarah's ex, her daughter's mom, is a close friend. While Pam, Sarah, and Sarah's ex did not get along at all in the early days, the three of them now have co-parented for many years and the ex maintains a close relationship with Pam and Sarah's daughter.

Pam and Sarah eventually divorced. Everyone still spent the holidays and birthdays together and kept their interpersonal relationships in place. Pam is now remarried, and her new partner, Ellen, has a seven-year-old son.

Now Pam's family is three households in two states. Most would expect her family would be just her, her wife and her children. But her family is fuller and, yes, more complicated than that. Don't be afraid to be honest about what your relationships look like. They don't need to be judged by anyone, and no one needs to approve them—except you and the people around you.

Whether your roommate is your next of kin or you're raising a sibling with the help of an ex-spouse, labels and identifiers don't matter. Value the relationships the best way you can, no matter how they were born.

For many of these abolitionist principles, I've made a notation that some of this work should be done with the help of trusted professionals, whether that's therapists, faith leaders or other qualified, objective people who understand your life and lifestyle. That's especially true with this one.

Strong abolitionist work is born of strong communities, and strong communities are born of strong interpersonal relationships. How you show up for yourself is how you show up for your community and how you show up for your work. It's all interconnected and interdependent.

There have been many times when movement work was affected—if not decimated—by individual personal problems. Whether it's drug addiction, financial problems or interpersonal relationships, it can and will come back to your community.

Huey P. Newton was the rock that created the Black Panther Party. Along with his co-leaders, he put actions in place that are still benefiting communities today, decades after the Black Panther Party was dismantled by Newton himself. Later, two women connected with the party were killed, and he was likely involved; he faced murder charges. He was eventually killed by a rival in a drug deal gone bad.

We know that the FBI's COINTELPRO infiltrated and sowed seeds of discord in organizations like the Black Panthers. But however it happens, it happens and our interpersonal relationships can be scarred, which can lead to our abolition work being affected.

How will you handle something like addiction in your ranks? How will you handle depression or other mental health issues with the people you value in your community? Will there be someone on call qualified to handle these things? Will you have a hands-off approach and encourage people to find help on their own?

Movement work tends to spill over into our personal lives. Colleagues often become family. We share stories of our lives and give examples of why we need to make change, and that makes us vulnerable. In order to have successful interpersonal relationships, you have to go into organizing thoughtfully and with a plan. The same way we plan for marriage or a long-term relationship, the same way we plan for a child: we think about worst-case scenarios, make emergency plans and watch for warning signs.

This all must be done with those we work with in abolitionist practice. If we value interpersonal relationships, it will show in our work.

What to Read/Watch/See/Hear: Read anything by Octavia Butler. The way Butler approached heartache,

hope, emotional density, protest, fight, power and practice is written from a place of devotion. You can feel the
love she has for the people she's writing about, especially
the women characters in her books. In all of her work,
the theme of valuing relationships comes through
clearly.

What I Know: There's a reason why this principle is
near the end. It's *hard.* It's one thing to keep your own
self together. It's something else entirely to value your
interpersonal relationships with multiple people and
try to make sure people see and feel that you care and
that you have their best interests and the relationship as
a whole in mind.

You'll need a whole lot of courageous conversations
for this one. Which is why we've been practicing this
since chapter one.

This one is another step that you need to do at the
granular level. You start with personality assessments
with the people in your movement. Who needs to meet
early? Who needs to meet as late as possible? Who
would be good at keeping a phone list for emergencies?
Who may not be able to show up for in-person meetings? Who is with child? Who has several children and
may need childcare in order to participate? Who is in
school? Who is in transitional housing? Who is looking
for employment? Who is overworked and underpaid?
This can go on and on. Movement work involves valuing interpersonal relationships, and that begins with
knowing your people.

Be willing to give of yourself, as well. You can't expect your interpersonal relationships to be valued if you don't do what you can to be open and honest about your own needs. Is the end of daylight saving time tough for you? Have you recently ended a relationship? We're not taught to go straight into a relationship with everything on the table. But we should do that. Both in our personal lives and our work as abolitionists. There's no room for not understanding one another when so much of what we do can be overwhelming and stressful at times.

Much of how we make this principle work depends on how we make the previous principles work.

Remember the cauldron? Well, community building and interpersonal relationships are similar. Keep them moving, keep an eye on them. Keep them warm, and don't let them burn or spill over. (Trust me, the analogy works!)

What You Know: You know who you are. You know what's important to you. You know your strengths and the things that challenge you. You know where you are in your journey as an abolitionist, and you know where you want to go.

Self-confidence and self-assurance are key to developing interpersonal relationships. You need them. The people working with you need to have them, as well.

Those Who Can Show: Cara Page is someone who lives her life in a way that helps us and others feel seen and heard. Just a peek into who she is and what she does gives us an example of fully showing up, being ready to begin and grow and value relationships, especially in work.

Cara is a curator and organizer who comes from a long line of organizers. She is Black, feminist and queer, and her work has involved liberation for people of color and transformative justice work with all kinds of healers. She focuses specifically on helping people work through generational trauma and changing policing and surveillance policies.

Her work is survivor led, and she believes in abolishing both the police system and the current medical system, neither of which work in conjunction with or for people of color and indigenous people. She studies the history of eugenics and medical experimentation, using uncomfortable conversation to shape the narrative on how the medical community has treated people of color and LGBTQIA+ communities.

Page regularly crisscrosses the country, sharing her work in art, writing and public speaking while also joining forces with other organizations and movements to share resources and ideas.

One of the many direct things we learn from Cara is the importance of naming that which makes us uncomfortable. That which has caused trauma, both direct and generational. If we want to build valuable relationships, we have to be able to identify that which must be healed or strengthened.

Cara cites such uncomfortable moments in her

creative narratives: "Listen You Can Hear the Mothers Crying in the Universe: A Black Feminist Poet's Requiem for Our Black Warrior Toni."

In the narrative, she discusses what it was like to grow up during the time of the Atlanta child murders. From 1979 to 1981, 28 young Black males were killed in the Atlanta area. The reporting was in-depth and horrendous, and Black parents nationwide, not just in the South, were absolutely terrified. Even up north and out west, Black parents were keeping their children home from school, especially after one victim was accosted while walking home from school.

In our communities, we have many traumatic stories to tell. We tend to shield our children as much as we can. But this time parents could not hide their terror. They were tucking their children in at night and telling them what was happening, not waiting until after bedtime and whispering to each other the way we sometimes do. It's now been 40 years. The parents who had children at that time and the children who were growing up at the time have never forgotten, and it is still part of our stories. When you look up and see your parents in tears, wishing they could move out of town, staring at the television and afraid to let you out of their sight, it stays with you. Page shares her experience and how it helped her understand how others process trauma.

Page also talks about the bombing of MOVE in Philadelphia. In 1985, the city of Philadelphia dropped a bomb from a helicopter on a settlement that housed MOVE, a militant political organization. Eleven people, including five children, died in the fire. It was national news. This was especially distressing for those who were doing movement work, as Cara Page's family was. There were constant skirmishes and clashes between movement workers and the police state.

If you were a young person growing up in the movement or just growing up Black and Brown in the United States in the 1970s and 1980s, these events shaped you. These events molded you. They connected you to others in your generation and in your community. You didn't forget the details, and you always thought about how you could have been affected—how it could have been you.

Drilling down on these things is what it means to develop a sense of self that can be a part of a community and a team.

These are just two examples. Imagine sitting across from your comrades in this work and everyone sharing their moments like this. Those who are baby boomers and Gen Xers, millennials and Zoomers have their own. Determining how we process these moments is what will help us form firm bonds.

Although we're still in the throes of the pandemic right now (and likely won't be all the way out of it when this book is in your hands), don't think for a moment that our youngest comrades won't come to us in need of understanding and healing. Many of them will have lost much of the pomp and circumstance and ceremony of formal education or have been thrust into complicated and radically different ways of learning, socializing and growing.

A friend recently told me that her 13-year-old hasn't seen her best friend's full face in eight months. They go to school together, six feet apart, every day. The idea is that you live life seeing *faces*. Having to strain to see laughter and smiles in people's eyes instead will affect us, all of us, especially our young folk.

We will have to be open with each other.

How We'll Grow: We'll journal. We'll sing. We'll dream. We'll indulge our creative side, no matter who can experience it, even if it's just for us. We'll talk to our people, we'll ask more questions and talk less. We'll develop our own style and support others in their journey to do the same. We'll read, read, read. Read to others and recommend reading. If we write, we'll write. If we don't, we'll write anyway. We'll talk. We'll listen. We'll nurture. We'll set boundaries. We'll recognize that sometimes, the best way to value a relationship is to let it go and close the door firmly. We'll recognize that the door can reopen for a different relationship with different boundaries. We'll show by opening our hearts to the possibilities of relationships we value.

The Real World: Several years ago, when BLM was still in its infancy, I did nothing else but work on this movement. I didn't see my friends or family, and my life was just head down in this work. I missed weddings I would have been into. I missed the births and birthdays of my godchildren. I was just completely gone. I wasn't a member of any personal communities, and my interpersonal relationships were trashed.

One spring day, I got a call from a very close friend. As soon as I saw her number, I cursed under my breath. I'd missed her birthday the day before. I answered the phone.

"Patrisse, this hurts."

"I know, Emmy. I am so sorry. I was at a meeting that ran late. I went home, got ready for your party and then fell asleep."

"Is that your excuse? You were at a meeting?"

I had to bite my lip from saying something mean. Didn't she understand what I was trying to create? Didn't she care?

So, in the real world, your close friends don't care. They shouldn't have to. You have a responsibility to show up for your friends and family the very best you can. It keeps you whole, and you'll need that. The movement is a living, breathing thing. So are your relationships with friends and family.

My friend Emmy forgave me. But our friendship has never quite been the same. We at least talk and see each other when we can. I had some friendships from the early days of BLM that just don't exist anymore. I'm talking about people I'd known and loved for decades. Don't let that happen. The real world has room for you and the movement.

GUIDING QUESTIONS

1. What is your most treasured interpersonal relationship? Describe it. Why is it your favorite? Why does it work?

2. Have you ever had to let go of a valued interpersonal relationship? How did you know when you couldn't value it the same anymore?

Fight the U.S. State Rather Than Make It Stronger

> Our strategy should be not only to confront the empire, but to lay siege to it. To deprive it of oxygen. To shame it. To mock it. With our art, our music, our literature, our stubbornness, our joy, our brilliance, our sheer relentlessness—and our ability to tell our own stories. Stories that are different from the ones we're being brainwashed to believe. The corporate revolution will collapse if we refuse to buy what they are selling—their ideas, their version of history, their wars, their weapons, their notion of inevitability. Remember this: We are many and they are few. They need us more than we need them. Another world is not only possible, she is on her way. On a quiet day, I can hear her breathing.
>
> —Arundhati Roy, *War Talk*

In its current form, the United States is a violent country with a brutal past and present. In her book of essays, *War Talk*, Arundhati Roy discusses racism and empire, war and peace and how they intersect.

There is no secret that the United States has wreaked havoc on its own citizens as well as communities and people across the world. Let's not forget slavery, indigenous genocide, the many wars the United States has initiated domestically and abroad, the inherent role it plays in profit over people. Our priorities are not in alignment with human dignity and creativity. U.S. current systems are in place to maintain the country's dominance through violence and profit. Part of the work we must do as abolitionists to get free is to create new avenues to undermine the current United States and the ability of its harmful, broken systems to further oppress, suppress and attack communities who are poor.

Let's dig into what Arundhati Roy suggests in the above quote, that we fight with "our art, our music, our literature, our stubbornness, our joy, our brilliance, our sheer relentlessness—and our ability to tell our own stories."

Our art has been a part of what has kept us whole for millennia and particularly since we were brought here as enslaved people.

A prime example of this would be the quilts of Gee's Bend, a semi-isolated Black community along the Alabama River. The women in the area, and their ancestors, are now known for their quilting.

Some of the quilters trace their ancestry to a place called Pettway Plantation, and some can name-check their ancestor, Dinah Miller, brought to the United States in 1859 on a slave ship.

Their work, brightly colored and geometrically patterned, is incredibly intricate, and the quilts are truly something special. One hundred years ago, they were made for warmth, not necessarily art. The quilters were using scraps of fabrics and pieces of clothing to create these vibrant quilts, handing down their methods generation to generation, through slavery, Jim Crow and the Civil Rights Movement.

After many years of being obscure, the quilters are now recognized as masters of the art of quilting and as contributing an immense wealth of art to American culture. Without changing their names or images for branding, selling their wares at white-owned galleries, moving from their hometown for larger cities, they began to sell their quilts, and they now travel the world as part of quilting exhibitions at national museums.

The women of Gee's Bend are an example of Roy's ideas. Their art held on, *they* held on. Because that art meant something to them, to their people, it is now appreciated worldwide. This is not to say that the women of Gee's Bend needed to have national recognition in order to matter. Quite the opposite: those who now know and experience the quilters' work, *they* now matter. That was not there. That was lost to them. It was never lost to the women in Gee's Bend.

This is how we live with our art and through our art. It is for our survival. If and when others bring it forth to the masses, it still belongs to us. We can still pass it down and hold it close.

John Bush, an eighteenth-century African soldier, carved horns used to store gunpowder. His carvings that survive are often noted for their intricate patterns and the calligraphy used for the text. Two hundred years later, John Bush is known. We can claim him. We can see what his skills were. Thinking about John Bush and the women quilters makes us wonder, what will we leave?

It may be fine arts.

It may also be an entirely new world. Our art may be dreaming up a world our forebears could not have imagined and putting it into place.

Our music holds us up and builds us up and has for centuries. If you truly know who we are and what we've been able to do, it's nothing short of astonishing. Music is absolutely the way we push back against racism, capitalism and patriarchy.

Art explains us. For example, music of the enslaved shows us that those in the Middle Passage were not stripped of all their traditions.

For years, we've created our own instruments, from drums and banjos to flutes and string instruments. Our development of music, how we delivered our vocals, was completely inventive; we created our own unique sound. From call and response, which would get passed down all the way through hip-hop, to melisma and vibrato. Our runs, our patterns, our tones, it's all ours. We've lent it out, for sure. But the richness of our art, including music, is how we hold on to our culture and use it in our work as abolitionists.

We can meet to map out our goals while swaying to

our sounds, admiring our art and creating a new genre altogether. All while smiling and enjoying our craft. Abolitionist work does not have to be done in the dark while breaking our backs and being miserable.

Yet, we also understand that our music, particularly in the eighteenth century, was more often a wail than a celebration. It is something we note, listen to, absorb, understand and honor. As abolitionists, we go toward the people in power knowing fully who we are and where we come from.

And our literature! We have held so deeply to our stories. We have passed down our words as poems, novels and songs, some published and some kept close. Our words, spoken and unspoken, have always been such a rich part of the fabric of our lives. From Phillis Wheatley in the 1700s, whose true story and true gifts we may never know, to the young people creating 30-second messages of hope and liberation for each other on social media.

For people often pulled apart from one another, Black and Brown people know how to communicate, and we use it as a first line of defense against many ills.

We can fight back against white supremacy. We already do it without even realizing it every day. Our art keeps this heart beating while we move.

Our families are also how we fight back and preserve our own stories and legacies. The concept of the nuclear family and the concept of marriage were originally tools to promote capitalism. Which is why the enslaved people in this country were not allowed to marry. The reasoning was that we did not need to advance in society, so there was no need to make our unions legally binding. We weren't going to own land or create generational wealth. So we created our own traditions, and it didn't stop us from creating families, then and now.

I'm not judging how anyone creates their families. I know that a nuclear family comes from a pro-capitalist white supremacist model, and disrupting that model doesn't mean that Black children won't have families. Families come in different shapes, sizes, relationships and viewpoints. How we create them should work for us—not for the government's constructs of what a family should look like.

There are states in this country that have laws on the books that ban how people love each other. The government literally can open your bedroom door and tell you that how you love another consenting adult is a crime. Abolitionist practice helps us break down this system, one day at a time.

What to Read/Watch/See/Hear: *The Purpose of Power: How We Come Together When We Fall Apart* by Alicia Garza. This book gives us instructions on how to be a part of the movement that is taking on the U.S. state. Alicia breaks down what is necessary for organizers and activists to come together under a government that consistently undermines and abuses marginalized communities. Alicia helps us think about the campaigns that will weaken white supremacy and strengthen the fight for social justice.

What I Know: Recently, I received a text message from an elder in the movement community. She said, simply, "I'm thinking about you during this time of tensions being exposed. I could have predicted. Hang in there and let me know if you need me." She was talking about the end of 2020, when several factions of BLM took their grievances public, including requesting my ousting.

That one text message was so uplifting, even without clear action steps. It reminded me how important it is to push back against the state and how we approach things from a state and governmental point of view. Conflict does not have to be drawn-out legal battles with lawyers reaping more money than any of the parties involved. Can I just ask an elder to interfere? Maybe not. But shouldn't the goal be to dismantle the agencies that keep us in their courtrooms, deciding our tensions? What can we do to make sure our battles are waged with courageous conversations, directly across from each other, with all the tears and emotion that come with that?

Listen, this part of the game is not easy. This is the part of the abolitionist practice where you join up with others. When I'm encouraging courageous conversation and imagining and leaning into feelings, yes, you can work on those principles alone and in small groups. But these are the heavy lifts and you can't do it alone. This is where building community and valuing interpersonal relationships begin to take shape and have meaning.

This is where it's time to identify where you are and what you want to work toward. Is it LGBTQIA+ issues? Is it animal rights? Is it the fight for clean water? Where do you live? What do you see right in front of you? What needs to change? People often ask me, "Where do I begin?" I say the same thing each time. You begin with where you are. For me, one of those early moments was getting bus passes into the hands of Los Angeles students. I knew those students. I knew those buses. I understood what needed to be done.

If you can't hit the streets or join an organization, amplify those who can. Right now, there are millions of protesters in India taking to the streets. It's not being reported in American media. Find out the details and become educated and amplify those voices.

Right now, in France, the authorities are resisting citizens filming arrests of any kind. These voices need to be amplified. Don't feel like you're not doing enough if you're not linked arm in arm on the front line. There is a time and place for that level of engagement, and you'll know if and when it's right for you.

There's another step you can take. If you don't see a movement or organization that's doing what's important to you—start one yourself.

What You Know: Let's keep it real. We know what we need to do to not make the United States stronger in terms of its racial policies and capitalist patriarchy.

But we also get mani-pedis.

We know our schools are not what we need them to be.

Some of us are also not in a place to homeschool and still have to get our kids educated.

We know the medical system has harmed us, continually, for centuries and continues to do so.

We also have to get the occasional filling and take our kids to the pediatrician.

We live here. We have to exist in this space, and we still have to find ways, large and small, to survive and yet push to thrive. We are human with the capacity to hold these contradictions. We can push ourselves to be uncomfortable in the name of not supporting white supremacy and a genocidal government.

And still cop that Ivy Park when it drops.

Those Who Can Show: Ida Bell Wells was born into slavery in 1862 in Holly Springs, Mississippi, to parents James Wells, a carpenter's apprentice, and Elizabeth Warrenton, a well-known cook in their town. When the Emancipation Proclamation was signed in 1863, Ida's parents became prominent advocates of education for the newly emancipated Black people during the Reconstruction Era. Ida grew up in a home that pushed education as a tool of liberation, but tragedy struck in 1878 when both her parents and a sibling died of yellow fever. Ida took on the responsibility of caring for her six remaining siblings and began her career, as it was for many educated women during that time, as a schoolteacher. She also had a passion for journalism and wrote articles for the local newspaper that were often centered around segregation and inequality.

She moved to Memphis, Tennessee, a few years later and was outraged by what she experienced in the Memphis education system. She wrote caustic articles about the Memphis Board of Education, critiquing the conditions of the Black schools of the city. Not surprisingly, Ida's teaching contract was not renewed, but her career as a journalist took off as she was hired on to write for various newspapers; the focus of her writing was on the injustices she was experiencing.

Ida's life in Memphis was flourishing, and by 1889 she was editor and co-owner with J. L. Fleming of *The Free Speech and Headlight*, a Black-owned newspaper. She was not only a prolific journalist but also a well-known actress in her town, grabbing the attention of a "dizzying" number of suitors who wanted to marry her. In her true feminist fashion, she was unwilling to marry just anyone, and at the age of 24, she wrote: "I will not begin at this late day by doing what my soul abhors; sugaring men, weak deceitful creatures, with flattery to retain them as escorts or to gratify a revenge." She found the ideals of equality and mutual respect in Ferdinand Barnett—a lawyer, journalist and Civil Rights activist. A trailblazer, Ida did not simply take his last name when they married—rather, she hyphenated her name (probably one of the first Black women to do so in that era!). Ida became a force to be reckoned with. In 1892, when her good friend Thomas Moss was lynched, it ignited her lifelong work as an anti-lynching activist.

Up until then, the official reports of the lynchings of Black men, much like the murders of Black people by police today, were largely accepted—the stories propagated the ideas that Black men were rapists threatening the safety and virginity of white women and that white vigilantes were just meting out justice to these Black criminals. When Moss, a Black grocery store owner, was lynched by a mob of white men after a confrontation at his store, Ida wrote a column in the newspaper about how the town of Memphis had failed to protect the lives and property of Black folks.

Moss was a co-owner of the People's Grocery, which was outperforming the white grocery store across the street. The white grocery owner went to the city council to complain about how this business was a "nuisance" to the town, and, essentially, the city council deputized men to get guns to go and "correct these business owners." When the white mob arrived, they were met by Black men who had rifles and were ready to defend themselves. There was a shoot-out in which some of the white men (who happened to be deputies) were injured, and the Black store owners were arrested and jailed. A few days later, the Black store owners were taken out of the courthouse and lynched by a white mob.

Ida wrote that the Black people in Memphis should all leave and head West because there was no justice for them in the city and that lynching was just a form of economic violence and terrorism. Ida became a target of white mob violence and was run out of Memphis. She relocated to Chicago, fleeing the terrors of the Jim Crow South—but not without bringing her supporters with her. Thousands of people left Memphis—about 5 percent of the population—and it crumbled the city's economy. Ida was not deterred, and became a journalist in exile as she traveled the South for two months, gathering information on other lynching incidents and writing about them in newspapers in graphic detail.

She single-handedly created the field of investigative journalism as she courageously visited the places where people had been tortured, shot, hanged and mutilated. She examined photos of victims, took sworn statements from eyewitnesses and studied local newspaper accounts. In 1895, she published a pamphlet, the "Red Record," the first statistical record of the history of American lynchings. Backed by data, Ida exposed the reality behind lynchings: they were largely used as economic retaliation. Her work grabbed international attention as she toured Europe and gave hundreds of lectures about the plight of Black people in America.

Ida openly confronted white women in the suffrage movement who did not take an intersectional stance— suffragettes who refused to talk about race and the rights of Black women, in particular, to vote. Because of her stance, Ida was often ridiculed and ostracized by (white) women's suffrage organizations in the United States, so she founded the National Association of

Colored Women's Club to address issues dealing with Civil Rights and women's suffrage. She was adamant that race, gender and liberation were not mutually exclusive issues. This woman did not compromise on her ideals—at the age of 68, she ran for a seat in the Illinois State Senate as an Independent just a decade after women won the right to vote in the United States.

Ida lived a self-actualized life—a world-renowned abolitionist, feminist, educator, and the mother of investigative journalism, she courageously challenged unjust systems during the Jim Crow era, when Black women did not have the vote or protection from the law. Her radical anti-lynching reporting changed the narrative of the mainstream media and exposed the corruption of the justice system. She was a strong proponent of self-ownership—she owned her mediums of communication (various newspapers), built institutions where people could educate themselves (the Black settlement houses for men and women) and created spaces where Black people could network (like the National Association of Colored Women's Club).

Ida understood that ownership gives you freedom to be your true authentic self, and she lived her life creating spaces where other Black people could cultivate their own liberation. She fought this country's oppressive systems tooth and nail, and her legacy as a fierce force of change and vision is a call to action for all of us to continue that work until we are free.

How We'll Grow: We're already doing it. Sometimes

as we push forward, the work can cloud our view of what we're accomplishing incrementally. As I write this, my four-year-old has mysteriously picked up a British accent from watching a bit of television on vacation. No matter what's going on in front of and around me, he can crack me up, and I know I'll help him develop his talents. I was a performer for my great-grandmother in much the same way. We're creating a much different world than the one she was born into.

Don't forget to look internally. Are you taking care of your health, not avoiding that cavity, making lunch instead of getting takeout? Listen: You are a freaking wonder. You are your ancestor's wildest, most courageous, visionary dream come to life. All that resilience in your DNA. Count that as a victory!

The Real World: This is it. This is now your space! This is *your* real world. You can use this section to record your work in all of the steps. Congratulations. This work has just begun.

GUIDING QUESTIONS

1. Map out three things you will do to ensure you fight for a country that truly supports its people.
2. What is one way you can fight the U.S. state?
3. How are you getting free?

Acknowledgments

This book is years in the making. It's a book I've been wanting to write for more than a decade. Many of us talk about abolition, but it's not often something we practice in our relationships. I see this work as a love note to humanity, and I'm so grateful for the folks who helped bring this practice to life.

Thank you Monique Patterson, my editor at St. Martin's Press, and the entire crew who helped give birth to this project. Your love, support and encouragement are so powerful. Victoria Sanders and Bernadette Baker-Baughman, my brilliant book agents who continue to help me be courageous through my writing.

Thanks to my manager Sarah Weichel and my PR team—Chelsea Thomas, Meredith O' Sullivan, Viveca Ortiz-Torres and Amanda Silverman at Lede Company for being such fierce and powerful women.

A special shout-out to the two women who ached over this book just as much as I did. Lissett Lazo, who helped shape the abolitionist biographies. Thank you Lissett for being such a grounding force in my life. And to Aliya King, who stepped in to support the shaping of this book and talked through abolition and transformative justice with me. You were the backbone of this project.

Thank you Melina Abdullah for being my sister in the struggle and pushing me to write and share my thoughts and pushing me in my leadership.

Thank you to all of my abolitionist practice partners. My community, organizations I support, and my chosen family. I see the possibility of abolition through our work.

Thank you in advance to folks who are reading this book, marking it up, feeling challenged by it and trying to contend with what abolition looks like in your intimate relationships and your political practice. This shit is really really really hard. But I promise you abolitionist practice is so worth it. I believe humanity deserves so much more than what we currently exist in. I believe we deserve care, and love, room to grow and make mistakes, and to be held in our desire to be better, stronger and freer.

Notes

3   **China has 1.7 million prisoners** World Prison Brief, "Highest to Lowest—Prison Population Total," https://www.prisonstudies.org/highest-to-lowest/prison-population-total?field_region_taxonomy_tid=All

3   **Hague Conventions** International Committee of the Red Cross, "Treaties, State Parties and Commentaries," https://ihl-databases.icrc.org/ihl/INTRO/150

5   **United States was the largest exporter of weapons from 2015 to 2019** Stockholm International Peace Research Institute, "SIPRI Arms Transfers Database," https://www.sipri.org/databases/armstransfers

5   **Egypt has received over $50 billion** U.S. Department of State, "U.S. Relations with Egypt," January 5, 2021, https://www.state.gov/u-s-relations-with-egypt/#:~:text=The%20United%20States%20established%20diplomatic,economic%20opportunity%2C%20and%20regional%20security

6   **U.S. military as one of the largest polluters** Benjamin Neimark, Oliver Belcher, and Patrick Bigger, "US Military Pollution," *Ecologist*, June 27, 2019, https://theecologist.org/2019/jun/27/us-military-pollution#:~:text=Greenhouse%20gas%20emission%20accounting%20usually,than%20most%20medium%2Dsized%20countries

6   **National Association for Mental Illness** "Jailing People with Mental Illness," NAMI, https://www.nami.org/Advocacy/Policy-Priorities/Divert-from-Justice-Involvement/Jailing-People-with-Mental-Illness

7   **musician using a streaming service?** Manatt, "How Streaming Services Pay Songwriters," Manatt.com, August 17, 2018, https://www.manatt.com/insights/news/2018/how-streaming-services-pay-songwriters

10   **12 steps to transforming yourself and the world** Patrisse Cullors, "Abolition and Reparations: Histories of Resistance, Transformative Justice, and Accountability," *Harvard Law Review*, April 10, 2019, https://harvardlawreview.org

/2019/04/abolition-and-reparations-histories-of-resistance
-transformative-justice-and-accountability/

32 Louis Till was killed due to "willful misconduct" "Mamie Till
Mobley," *The American Experience*, https://www.pbs.org/wgbh
/americanexperience/features/emmett-biography-mamie
-till-mobley/

32 Recent investigations made by writer John Edgar Wideman
John Edgar Wideman, *Writing to Save a Life: The Louis Till File*
(New York: Scribner, 2016).

32 She recounts History.com Editors, "Emmett Till," history.com,
December 2, 2009, https://www.history.com/.amp/topics
/black-history/emmett-till-1

32 heirloom left to Emmett from his father youtube.com,
https://www.youtube.com/watch?v=tZpDU7uarTw

34 strategize with leaders Sarah Pruitt, "How Emmett Till's Murder Galvanized the Civil Rights Movement," history.com,
February 3, 2017, https://www.history.com/news/new-book
-sheds-light-on-the-murder-of-emmett-till-the-civil-rights
-movement

34 67 minutes of deliberation "The Trial of J.W. Milam and Roy
Bryant," *The American Experience*, https://www.pbs.org/wgbh
/americanexperience/features/emmett-trial-jw-milam-and
-roy-bryant/

35 one of her memorable speeches Rebekah Buchanan, "The
Heroism and Activism of Mamie Till Mobley," Tri States Public Radio, September 3, 2015, https://www.tspr.org/post
/heroism-and-activism-mamie-till-mobley

45 Malcolm X discussed the March on Washington *The Autobiography of Malcolm X, As Told to Alex Haley* (New York: Grove
Press, 1966).

50 Toni Morrison did an interview "Toni Morrison-intro
and interview," YouTube, https://www.youtube.com
/watch?v=WoTELoC8Q0M&t=643s

59 Dream Defenders https://dreamdefenders.org/our-story/

60 He tried to negotiate his time "Phillip Agnew: March on
Washington Dream Defenders Leader Cut from March Puts
Out Video," CBMA, https://blackmaleachievement.org/blog
/phillip-agnew-march-on-washington-dream-defenders
-leader-cut-from-march-puts-out-video

63 art as integral to organizing Aja Monet and Phillip Agnew, "A Love Story About the Power of Art as Organizing,"

TEDWomen 2018, https://www.ted.com/talks/aja_monet
_and_phillip_agnew_a_love_story_about_the_power_of_art
_as_organizing?language=en

63 **Black Men Build** "Wartime: Black Men's Survival Guide, Part One," June 2020, https://drive.google.com/file/d/1DQwipQ LdigXIgjD3r9h8JFwMBcRjCosM/vie

78 **6,000 thoughts every day** Anne Craig, "Discovery of 'Thought Worms' Opens Window to the Mind," *Queen's Gazette*, July 13, 2020, https://www.queensu.ca/gazette/stories/discovery -thought-worms-opens-window-mind

80 **"the all-purpose use of cages to solve social, political and economic problems"** Pamela J. Johnson, "Portrait of an Activist-Academic," USC Dornsife, October 1, 2006, https://dornsife .usc.edu/news/stories/223/portrait-of-an-activist-academic/

81 **carceral geography** Rachel Kushner, "Is Prison Necessary? Ruth Wilson Gilmore Might Change Your Mind," *New York Times Magazine*, April 17, 2019, https://www.nytimes.com /2019/04/17/magazine/prison-abolition-ruth-wilson -gilmore.html

81 **1 percent annual decline in the US prison population** Nazgol Ghandnoosh, "U.S. Prison Population Trends," *The Sentencing Project*, https://www.sentencingproject.org /publications/u-s-prison-population-trends-massive-build- up-and-modest-decline/

81 **Critical Resistance** http://criticalresistance.org/about /history/

90 **70 percent of NFL players** Robert W. Turner II, *Not for Long* (New York: Oxford University Press, 2018).

95 **James Baldwin and Nikki Giovanni met and spoke for hours** Soul, "Full Conversation with James Baldwin and Nikki Giovanni in London, 1971, Part I," https://www.youtube.com /watch?v=KL_cM7SXfbo; Soul, "Full Conversation with James Baldwin and Nikki Giovanni in London, 1971, Part II," https://www.youtube.com/watch?v=P1mK1a_198o

98 **1972 book** *No Name in the Street* James Baldwin, *No Name in the Street* (New York: Vintage Books, 2007.

99 **Baldwin had almost two thousand** F.B. Eyes Digital Archive, "James Baldwin," http://omeka.wustl.edu/omeka/exhibits /show/fbeyes/baldwin; F.B. Eyes Digital Archive, "Richard Wright," http://omeka.wustl.edu/omeka/exhibits/show /fbeyes/wright

99   **Toni Morrison eulogized him** Toni Morrison, "James Baldwin: His Voice Remembered; Life in His Language," *New York Times*, December 20, 1987, https://archive.nytimes.com/www.nytimes.com/books/98/03/29/specials/baldwin-morrison.html?utm_campaign=pubexchange_article&utm_medium=referral&utm_source=huffingtonpost.com

102 **adrienne maree brown** "Generation Mixed: Breaking the Race Barrier," *Yes Magazine*, March 5, 2010, https://www.yesmagazine.org/issue/america-remix/opinion/2010/03/05/generation-mixed-breaking-the-race-barrier/

102 **"guideline of her life"** https://www.youtube.com/watch?v=n0eI9jJRGyk&feature=youtu.be

102 **military environment** https://www.modeldmedia.com/features/lgbtleader112.aspx

104 **"human beings always choose the path of pleasure"** adrienne maree brown, *Pleasure Activism: The Politics of Feeling Good (Emergent Strategy)* (Chico, CA: AK Press, 2019).

104 **"practice variance"** brown, *Pleasure Activism.*

115 **BadAss Visionary Healers** BadAss Visionary Healers, "Babeilicious Healing Justice Statement," *nineteen sixty nine: an ethnic studies journal* 2 (1), 2013.

127 **schools remained segregated** "John Lewis Biography," biography.com, https://www.biography.com/political-figure/john-lewis

129 **arrested 40 times** Michael A. Fletcher, "I Didn't Understand John Lewis at First," The Undefeated, July 18, 2020, https://theundefeated.com/features/i-didnt-understand-john-lewis-civil-rights-leader-at-first/

129 **"move toward reconciliation"** David Cohen, "John Lewis, Civil Rights Icon and Longtime Congressman, Dies," *Politico*, July 17, 2020, https://www.politico.com/news/2020/07/17/john-lewis-obit-civil-rights-congress-036212

129 **"apology heard 'round the world"** John M. Glionna, "Great Read: Police Chief's Apology Sows Healing, Friendship," *Los Angeles Times*, September 23, 2014, https://www.latimes.com/nation/la-na-c1-civil-rights-friends-20140923-story.html

162 **one-third to one-half of all people murdered by police are disabled and/or deaf people or have mental health issues** Abigail Abrams, "Black, Disabled and at Risk: The Overlooked Problem of Police Violence Against Americans with

Disabilities," *Time*, June 25, 2020, https://time.com/5857438/police-violence-black-disabled/

163 **accomplices to disabled folks** Leah Lakshmi Piepzna-Samarasinha, "Cripping the Resistance," Disability Visibility Project, n.d., https://disabilityvisibilityproject.com/2020/08/24/cripping-the-resistance-no-revolution-without-us/?fbclid=IwAR31AZlXgGqUZMzFbe5gSd3v8Q5i_IoVIYccAxBGyGPoIo1FnxIJqV5GzuA

163 **right to self-determination** generation FIVE, "What Are Community Accountability & Transformative Justice?" Transformative Justice Kollektiv Berlin, https://www.transformativejustice.eu/en/what-are-ca-and-tj/

170 **California prisons sterilized hundreds of women as recently as 2010** Shilpa Jindia, "Belly of the Beast: California's Dark History of Forced Sterilizations," *Guardian*, June 30, 2020, https://www.theguardian.com/us-news/2020/jun/30/california-prisons-forced-sterilizations-belly-beast; and Eleanor Brock, "The Truth About Women of Color Behind Bars," *logikcull*, September 25, 2018, https://www.logikcull.com/blog/women-color-behind-bars

170 **Many states phased out these procedures in the 1970s** Lea Hunter, "The US Is Still Forcibly Sterilizing Prisoners," Talk Poverty, August 23, 2017, https:/talkpoverty.org/2017/08/23/u-s-still-forcibly-sterilizing-prisoners/

172 **Prince Edward County** Christopher Bonastia, "The Ugly Segregationist History of the Charter School Movement," Salon, January 7, 2015, https://www.salon.com/2015/01/07/the_ugly_segregationist_history_of_the_charter_school_movement_partner/

175 **"about survivorhood, disability justice"** https://micemagazine.ca/author/leah-lakshmi-piepzna-samarasinha

179 **We also know that heavy use of social media can lead to depression** HelpGuide, "Social Media and Mental Health," HelpGuide, https://www.helpguide.org/articles/mental-health/social-media-and-mental-health.htm

188 **Kevin Spacey** Bill Chappell, "Kevin Spacey Apologizes To Anthony Rapp Over Alleged Sexual Misconduct," NPR, October 30, 2017, https://www.npr.org/sections/thetwo-way/2017/10/30/560779174/kevin-spacey-apologizes-to-anthony-rapp-over-alleged-sexual-misconduct

191   **Congressman Joe Barton** Robert M. Eisinger, "The Political
      Non-Apology," *Society* 48 (March 2011), https://go.gale.com
      /ps/anonymous?id=GALE%7CA360204825&sid=google-
      Scholar&v=2.1&it=r&linkaccess=abs&issn=01472011&p=A-
      ONE&sw=w

191   **Tiger Woods** Deron Snyder, "Tiger Said All He Needed To
      Say," The Root, February 20, 2010, https://www.theroot.com
      /tiger-said-all-he-needed-to-say-1790878674

193   **Commander Jon Burge** Associated Press, "Ex-Chicago Police
      Commander Linked to Torture of More than 100 Suspects
      Dies," *Guardian*, September 19, 2018, https://www.theguardian.
      com/us-news/2018/sep/19/chicago-cop-jon-burge-torture-dies

194   **Disability justice** "Mia Mingus on Disability Justice," inter-
      viewed by Greg Macdougall, Equitable Education Media,
      November 30, 2013, https://www.youtube.com/watch?v
      =3cJkUazW-jw&feature=youtu.b

197   **"[i]f we cannot handle the small things between us"** "The
      Four Parts of Accountability," *Leaving Evidence*, December
      18, 2019, https://leavingevidence.wordpress.com/2019/12
      /18/how-to-give-a-good-apology-part-1-the-four-parts-of
      -accountability/

205   **study done with thousands of officers showed an insignificant
      difference** Lindsey Van Ness, "Body Cameras May Not Be the
      Easy Answer Everyone Was Looking For," Pew, January 14,
      2020, https://www.pewtrusts.org/en/research-and-analysis
      /blogs/stateline/2020/01/14/body-cameras-may-not-be-the
      -easy-answer-everyone-was-looking-for

208   *Locking Up Our Own* James Forman Jr., *Locking Up Our Own:
      Crime and Punishment in Black America* (New York: Farrar,
      Straus and Giroux, 2017).

226   **being pulled out of his car at gunpoint** Jourdain Searles, "In-
      secure's Kendrick Sampson Knows 'There Is No Revolution
      Without Art,'" *Vulture*, June 18, 2020, https://www.vulture
      .com/article/kendrick-sampson-interview-insecure-miss
      -juneteenth-blm-protests.html

227   **BLD PWR** https://www.bldpwr.com

227   **"[Hollywood is] actually an oppressive capitalist, white su-
      premacist system"** Mik Awake, "The Liberated Life of Ken-
      drick Sampson," *GQ*, June 19, 2020, https://www.gq.com/story
      /kendrick-sampson-juneteenth-profile

238 **Cara Page is** Barnard Center for Research on Women, "Cara Page," https://bcrw.barnard.edu/fellows/cara-page/

250 **Alicia Garza** Alicia Garza, *The Purpose of Power: How We Come Together When We Fall Apart* (New York: One World, 2020).

253 **Ida Bell Wells** Arlisha R. Norwood, "Ida B. Wells-Barnett," National Women's History Museum, 2017, https://www.womenshistory.org/education-resources/biographies/ida-b-wells-barnett

254 **"dizzying" number of suitors** Ida B. Wells, *Crusade for Justice: The Autobiography of Ida B. Wells*, 2nd edition (Chicago: University of Chicago Press, 1970, 2020).

255 **Thomas Moss** "The People's Grocery Lynchings (Thomas Moss, Will Stewart, Calvin McDowell)," Lynching Sites Project, Memphis, https://lynchingsitesmem.org/lynching/peoples-grocery-lynchings-thomas-moss-will-stewart-calvin-mcdowell

256 **"Red Record"** David Smith, "Ida B Wells: The Unsung Heroine of the Civil Rights Movement," *Guardian*, April 27, 2018, https://www.theguardian.com/world/2018/apr/27/ida-b-wells-civil-rights-movement-reporter

257 **a strong proponent of self-ownership** "Foremothers | Day 15 | Ida B. Wells," GirlTrek's Black History Bootcamp, June 2020, https://open.spotify.com/episode/2u5xoM2dPdP79s4NICNhk0?si=tOG37Sm5Qo6ZtRLOK40f6Q&context=spotify%3Ashow%3A3V3oyvy07Z9Q4fdYlc8mC6&nd=1